Reflections on a Life in Social Work

A Personal & Professional Memoir

Olive Stevenson

HINTONHOUSE

First published in 2013 by
Hinton House Publishers Ltd,
Newman House,
4 High Street,
Buckingham, MK18 1NT, UK

T +44 (0)1280 822557
F +44 (0)560 3135274
E info@hintonpublishers.com
www.hintonpublishers.com

British Library Cataloguing in Publication Data
A CIP catalogue record for this book is available from the British Library.

ISBN 978 1 906531577

Printed and bound in the United Kingdom by Hobbs the Printers Ltd.

Reflections on a Life in Social Work

Contents

Acknowledgements   vii

Preface   ix
    Professor Phyllida Parsloe & Sara Glennie Shevenell

Foreword   Olive Stevenson: A Life in Social Work Well Lived   xi
    Professor Harry Ferguson

Introduction   1

1   Early Years & Influences   3

2   Reflections on Health & Healthcare   13

3   Early Interest in Social Work   19

4   Becoming a Social Worker   23

5   Life as a Social Worker   31

6   Further Professional Development   41

7   A Social Work Academic: Early Years   45

8   The Maria Colwell Inquiry   61

9   Unresolved Issues for Social Work   69

References   83

Appendix I   85
   Direct Work with Children: The Relevance of Clare
   Winnicott's Teaching to Contemporary Social Work Practice

Appendix II   101
   The 1999 Graham Lecture 'Growing Older: What is it Like?'

Postscript   125
   Jane Campbell

Bibliography   127
   Published Works by Olive Stevenson

Acknowledgements

Olive would like to thank Sara Glennie Shevenell for helping to lift the manuscript from her desk, Miranda Robson for her careful editing and Sarah Miles of Hinton House Publishers, for providing all the encouragement and support necessary to achieve publication.

Preface

In October 2010 a severe stroke halted progress on this partially completed personal and professional memoir. Olive had been working on it, alongside the construction of her website (www. olivestevenson.com), as she approached retirement at the age of eighty. Her motivation was two-fold. Personally, the memoir provided a framework within which Olive could openly explore important questions about the connections between her early life experience and her subsequent choice of profession; in that sense this account shares with other memoirs a reflective and integrative quality. Professionally, Olive recognised her almost unique position of having been actively involved in social work for more than sixty years. 'Someday, someone will want to write a history of social work in the UK,' she said, recognising that her experience and perspective may be of value in the compilation of such a history. In that sense, this book is an important historical document, outlining as it does some of the key debates that have characterised the development of social work in the UK. It also reminds us, through poignant stories of her early work as a Child Care Officer, that whilst the detail of social work practice has changed significantly, its core values are enduring.

Although no longer able to write as she once did, Olive reviewed her partially written manuscript with the help of friends and agreed that, although incomplete, it was important to attempt publication. Harry Ferguson has ably set Olive's work in context. His spirited introduction grapples successfully with the difficulties associated with a selective and partial account. He not only fills in some of the gaps in Olive's extraordinary career but explores some of the ideas she introduces and relates them directly to current social work practice and policy context. The two appended lectures, written in the clear voice that many will recognise, identify the key issues that preoccupied Olive during the latter part of her working life.

Jane Campbell's sensitive and revealing Postscript confirms Olive's life-long commitment to critical reflection and sheds light on the reasons why she may have chosen to write about some aspects of her multifaceted career and to exclude others. Along with all the other things that this book may be, and each reader will take something different from it, Olive provides direct evidence of the importance of engaging in some form of sense-making as we age and begin the process of letting go of parts of life that have been so vital and defining.

Professor Phyllida Parsloe
Sara Glennie Shevenell
2013

Foreword

Olive Stevenson:
A Life in Social Work Well Lived

When the history of British social work in the twentieth and early twenty-first centuries is written the presence and contribution of Olive Stevenson will loom large. In a remarkable career spanning from the late 1940s through to the first years of the 2000s, Olive Stevenson's contribution to social work as a practitioner, teacher, researcher, scholar and consultant has been truly immense. She was without doubt the leading social work academic of her generation.

This invaluable memoir relates the story of Olive's life and her sixty years in social work, which began at the age of seventeen when she got a job as an 'assistant house mother' in a children's home in Croydon, London. She officially retired as Professor of Social Work at the University of Nottingham in 1994, but while she took the title of Emeritus Professor of Social Work, Olive's work rate remained extraordinary as she continued to teach, supervise PhD students, research, write, do consultancy, give public lectures and do public service work, which included sitting on and chairing many committees. Olive finally stopped teaching at the university in 2010, while still keeping her scholarship and public speaking going. In 2009, for instance, at the age of 79, Olive gave a wonderful public lecture at the University of Nottingham on the work of social work academic Clare Winnicott, her former mentor at the

London School of Economics (LSE). All of the attributes that made Olive so effective, successful and popular were on display: her intellectual power, communication skills, passion, emotional intelligence, practice wisdom, and her wit. This lecture is reproduced in Appendix I of this volume.

This memoir gives a good flavour of the sheer scope and range of Olive's contributions. My colleague in the Centre for Social Work at the University of Nottingham, Marian Charles, who has known Olive for more than 25 years, including time working as her research assistant in the 1980s and 1990s, relates many stories about just how much in demand Olive always was. However, this memoir only partially records the scale of Olive's productivity and output. There are several possible reasons for this. It may in part be due to modesty, or more likely a desire to focus less on some of the detail of achievements and more on the lived experience and how it all felt. It also exposes perhaps some of the limits of autobiography as a form in which the writer can never see themselves as we readers do, or necessarily dwell on the stories that interest us most, or entirely be what we want them to be. For instance, Olive was the founding editor of the *British Journal of Social Work* in 1971, which has long been by far the most important academic social work journal in Britain and among the highest ranked in the English speaking world. In this book Olive makes virtually nothing of that achievement – not, I suspect, because she does not recognise its importance or is not proud of it, more that within the flow of a professional life it was taken in her stride as just one thing among many and little fuss made of it. Then, at a practical level, there was the impact of Olive's ill-health which struck before she had brought the manuscript to completion and which denied her the opportunity to add further detail in making the final touches to the book. It was against this background that I was asked to provide an introduction that summarises Olive's contribution and offers an assessment of it in the wider context of social work history and knowledge.

Olive's Career in Social Work

I will begin with an overview of Olive's career. This is not meant to be definitive in the sense of covering every detail but is intended to compliment what Olive has written in the memoir, especially with respect to areas where there are some gaps.

Olive completed her undergraduate studies at the University of Oxford and went on to do her social work training at the LSE (1952/1953). After some five years in practice she did the Advanced Social Casework course at the Tavistock Clinic in London (1958/1959). In 1959 she took up her first academic post, at the University of Bristol and during her career held posts at three more universities: Oxford, 1962–1976; Keele, 1976–1983; and Nottingham, 1984–1994/2010. Over the years she researched and taught on fostering and adoption, children in care, child abuse and neglect, child protection, inter-agency working, adult abuse and safeguarding vulnerable adults. She published her first book, *Someone Else's Child: A Book for Foster Parents* in 1964 and during her career wrote or co-wrote at least eleven books. There were dozens more journal articles, book chapters and research reports. (See the Bibliography for a full list of Olive's published work.) Her 1973 book, *Claimant or Client*, was a product of time spent as a Social Worker Advisor to the Supplementary Benefits Commission and she regarded the issues it dealt with as being of great significance to social policy in general and not just social security.

Saul Becker, now Professor of Social Policy and Social Work at The University of Nottingham, recalls how influential *Claimant or Client* was on his PhD in the mid-1980s and on his subsequent research and publications concerning social work and poverty:

> I was at Nottingham at the time. Olive would discuss with me my ideas and she encouraged me to develop my thinking and research on 'poor clients'. Later, when I moved my research focus to 'young carers' Olive continued to encourage me and give me a platform. She instinctively recognised 'new' issues and challenges for social work thinking, policy and practice.

The first 'mainstream' book, *Young Carers and Their Families*, (Becker et al, 1998) was commissioned by Olive and published in her series for Blackwell Science.

A striking feature of Olive's work is how grounded it always was in empirical research into policy and practice. In the 1970s she turned her attention to inquiring into the changing role of social work within what were then newly constituted Local Authority Social Services Departments and in 1978, with Phyllida Parsloe, published *Social Service Teams: The Practitioner's View*. Commissioned by the (then) Department of Health and Social Security, it examined the task of the field worker within local authority social services departments and their equivalents in Scotland and Northern Ireland and considered the implications for social work education.

In 1973/1974 Olive was a member of the inquiry team that examined the circumstances surrounding the death from abuse of seven-year-old Maria Colwell in Brighton (Department of Health and Social Security, 1974). As she makes plain in this memoir, this involvement was to have a huge impact on her career and to an extent that she even expresses a certain regret at the 'celebrity status' she felt she reluctantly acquired following her role in the inquiry. Unhappy with the interpretations of the evidence by the Committee and what she viewed as its simplistic understanding of social work, she wrote a minority report. She points out in this book that she actually also wrote the section of the main report on inter-professional working. There is a huge literature today on the need for professionals to work together and communicate if child protection is to be effective. It is crucial to bear in mind that Olive was researching and writing about such issues at a time when little knowledge was available. Procedures and practices such as case conferences in child protection work are taken for granted today and the research Olive did with Christine Hallett was pioneering in shedding light on these complex processes and promoting evidence-based policy development. Olive and Christine's 1980 book, *Child Abuse: Aspects of Inter-professional Communication*, was for many years a core text not just on social work courses but across all disciplines concerned with child welfare.

Many more research reports and training initiatives followed. At the University of Nottingham, Marian Charles was appointed as Olive's research assistant in 1988 to work on a then Department of Health grant to develop training materials for inter-professional work in child protection. That led to the establishment of what was called the Professional Development Group, which also included Barbara Firth and Sara Glennie Shevenell and was led by Olive. The work and writing it spawned was considerable and included Olive becoming amongst the first influential Independent Chairs of a local authority Area Child Protection Committee (now Local Safeguarding Boards). These are key inter-agency meetings at which high-risk cases and local child protection policies and processes are reviewed. During a period in the 1990s Olive chaired four Area Child Protection Committees in different parts of the country at the same time! This added further to her great contribution (research, writing and passionate promotion) to work on behalf of neglected children in particular and her 1998 book, *Neglected Children: Issues and Dilemmas*, a second edition of which was published in 2007. The work on child neglect also enabled Olive to make the link with vulnerable adults, and in the late 1990s and 2000s her concern for issues such as the abuse of older people matured into a distinctive contribution in its own right. The research she did was typified by a highly original study with Katharine Jeary (2004) into 'The sexual abuse of elderly people – its distinctive characteristics and implications for policy and practice' and in 2008, for instance, she published in the *Journal of Adult Protection* on 'Neglect as an aspect of the mistreatment of elderly people'.

Olive's public service roles included Social Work Advisor at the Supplementary Benefits Commission (1968). She was also a member of the Social Security Advisory Committee (1980–2000), where she helped to shape a humane approach to cold weather payments to elderly and disabled people. Later in her career and during 'retirement' in the 1990s and 2000s, she was for many years also a Trustee and later Chair of Trustees of the Ann Craft Trust (ACT) an organisation based in the University of Nottingham that provides expertise, advocacy and training in relation to safeguarding adults with learning disabilities. Deborah Kitson, who was taught by Olive at Nottingham University in the early 1980s and is now Director of ACT, emphasises the huge commitment Olive made to the organisation's work and in speaking at their conferences. Deborah recalls: 'So many people locally loved to hear Olive speak at conferences. I never knew her to use Power Point etc, and she always spoke with passion and humility.'

Olive's leadership is evident in how she achieved a series of firsts. She was the first woman to be appointed to a professorship at the University of Keele. As already alluded to, she was a member of the inquiry committee that examined the death from abuse of seven-year-old Maria Colwell in Brighton in 1973, the first ever public inquiry of its kind in the UK. In the 40 years since, inquiries of this kind have become hugely significant in shaping the nature of social work. Such was the importance of the case that to this day it continues to be the subject of articles and entire books (Parton, 2004; Butler & Drakeford, 2011). The importance of Olive's contribution as the first editor of the *British Journal of Social Work* cannot be over-exaggerated. Her life-long professionalism, scholarly rigour and vision as an academic leader shine through in the first editorial she wrote in the first-ever edition of the journal in 1971:

> The first edition of the *British Journal of Social Work* is something of an event. I have no intention of writing lengthy editorials in subsequent editions. The journal must speak for itself and justify – or fail to justify – its claim to be a 'learned journal', comparable to other professions and academic disciplines. ... It is hoped to strike a balance in the Journal between three kinds of article. First it is our intention to publish research, relevant to social work, designed and executed with proper regard to techniques of social research now available. ... If work claims to be 'research' then it must be judged by rigorous standards. However, social work will always profit from a second category of writing – that of good description – even if it cannot claim statistical validity and can do no more than point up interesting issues for further study. ... Then thirdly there is always room for reflection and argument. Frances Drake's presidential address to the Children's Officer's Association has been included

for this reason. There is a need to spend time looking at the trees
(or even the leaves of the trees) with suitable scientific precision but
there is also a need to look at the wood, if we are not to lose our way.

(Stevenson, 1971, pp.1–3)

This shows once again just how important Olive was to laying the
foundations for social work as a respected, research-informed
academic discipline, while ensuring that it remained relevant to the
learning needs of practitioners and the developmental needs of the
profession.

Along with all the above activity Olive was also carrying out
administrative duties and, as her career progressed, senior
management responsibilities within the universities where she
worked. For instance, while Professor of Social Work Studies at the
University of Nottingham, 1984–1994, between 1987–1991 she
was head of the combined School of Sociology, Social Policy and
Social Work. The recollections of one colleague, Dr Mark Lymbery,
Associate Professor of Social Work at the University of Nottingham,
typify the role Olive played in the development of countless
academic careers:

> I was interviewed by her (and others) for a post in Notts Social
> Services Department Training Section in 1986 and was appointed as
> the liaison between the Social Services Department and various social
> work courses at that point. She maintained something of a nurturing
> and developmental brief on my career thereafter; I was brought in
> to teach on various parts of the programme by her, for example. She
> also helped me to make a transition into being a published writer.
> One of my early faltering pieces she declared, 'beautifully typed'. I
> was inordinately pleased by this and could therefore engage with her
> more substantive criticisms. It was only a few days later that I realised
> that her apparent compliment said nothing about the quality of the
> piece at all!

Olive also made a significant contribution to social work
internationally. From the early 1980s she became actively involved
in the development of social work in Hong Kong and China. She
supervised the PhDs of a number of academic staff from the Poly-
University of Hong Kong, where she was made an Honorary

Professor in 2004 and was also active in the nascent development of social work at Peking University in China.

Olive's achievements and huge contribution to social work, social policy and public life were recognised through the award of honours. In 1994 she was awarded a CBE in the Queen's Birthday Honours. In 1996 she received an Honorary Doctorate from the University of East Anglia, and the University of Kingston awarded her an Honorary Doctorate in 2005.

The striking thing about Olive's career when viewed in the round is the sheer scale and variety of the roles she played and the contributions she made. It bears emphasising then that, while deeply scholarly, she was far from being an orthodox academic. Because she played such a crucial role in public life, Olive was in fact a public intellectual.

Olive's Contribution to Social Work

This memoir is not only of value for the insights it gives us into the life in social work of a remarkably influential individual, however. It is of vital importance to the profession of social work, and for three reasons. First, it provides a unique historical record of social work from its formative period as a modern profession after the Second World War. Owing to the length of Olive's career the book covers events and developments in organisations, theory, policy, and practice that were formative of the profession today. It is a mine of information about the big events Olive was involved in and developments in social work she lived through, such as the setting up of unified social services departments in the early 1970s, and the impact of the Maria Colwell Inquiry. Crucial insights are given into the spirit of times past and the status and nature of social work as a social and political project within the burgeoning welfare state. Speaking of her experience as a social work student at LSE in 1952/1953 where she was taught and mentored by Clare and Donald Winnicott, Olive writes of herself and fellow students: 'We were people whose clear task was to raise standards of child welfare in the country.' What light, we need to ask ourselves, does the optimism and professional faith in social work embedded in that vision shed on the much more troubled social status of social work today? How might such a vision be recaptured? Then there are the recollections provided of the small but vitally important details of how social work was done and professional identity managed. For instance, students and practitioners today will be intrigued to learn of the ease with which, in the 1950s and 1960s, home telephone numbers were given out to service users.

Secondly, this is a valuable text for social work because it is a personal as well as a professional account of living and working in the profession in a context where there are remarkably few biographical accounts of people involved in British social work (exceptions are Joel Kanter [2004] on Clare Winnicott, Kathleen Jones [1984] on Eileen Younghusband and Judith Niechcial's [2010] book on Lucy Faithful, for which Olive wrote a foreword). This memoir shows the ways in which early experiences in the family and a range of biographical factors shape social workers as practitioners and academics, leading to a lifetime commitment to public service. Olive writes openly and honestly about her sexuality and emphasises the importance of friendships and how they were inextricably bound up with work, paying tribute to some of her closest and oldest friends, especially Phyllida Parsloe with whom she shared a house (and some cases!) when they were newly qualified social workers in Devon. Phyllida also went on to become an eminent academic and researched and wrote with Olive (Parsloe & Stevenson, 1978).

Thirdly, this memoir is of vital importance for its theoretical contribution to social work and in how it charts an intellectual contribution and legacy that resonates throughout social work today. Olive's particular vision is perhaps best captured in this book where she writes: 'How best, in seeking to help others, to use one's mind and one's feelings, has remained a central preoccupation of my professional life.' What needs to be grasped is how Olive was a central figure in the formation of ideas and theory that remain central to social work and child welfare practice today. It is a matter of common knowledge, amongst lay people as well as professionals that children need a cuddly toy, blanket or some other 'transitional object' to help them emotionally to make changes, like going to bed or taking a journey. It was in a 1954 paper that Donald Winnicott coined the notion of the 'transitional object' (Winnicott, 1951). Olive relates here how in her LSE research dissertation she explored its relevance to a sample of infants and to her amazement as a student it was published in a scholarly journal (Stevenson, 1954). What she doesn't point out is that in his classic 1971 book, *Playing and Reality*, where he deepens his analysis of the transitional object concept, Donald Winnicott duly acknowledges the important contribution that Olive's research made to his thinking and the need for further empirical research of the kind she had conducted (Winnicott, 1971, p.xii).

Olive was a pioneer in the use of psychoanalytic concepts in social work. This reflects the influence of the teachers and mentors with whom she chose to surround herself were some of the towering names in applied psychoanalytic thought, such as John Bowlby and Clare and Donald Winnicott. During her Advanced Social Work training at the Tavistock Clinic (1958/1959) she formed a close friendship with Isca Wittenberg-Salzberger, who was then training to become a psychoanalyst (and went on to have a distinguished career working at the Tavistock Clinic) and who, in 1970, published what became a social-work classic, *Psychoanalytic Insight and relationships: A Kleinian Approach* (Wittenberg-Salzberger, 1970). Olive was even once a guest at the London home of Anna Freud, the youngest daughter of Sigmund Freud, and writes humorously in this book about that occasion during which she gave a seminar paper to Anna and her friends and colleagues while quaking in her boots.

It would, however, be a grave mistake to allow this to conjure up images of Olive helping to train intense psychoanalytic social workers whose clients were seen 'on the couch'. She recalls in this book how on becoming a social work educator in the late 1950s and early 1960s, she 'flung' herself into the tutorial role and how 'Fresh from the Tavistock, I was rather too preoccupied with the unconscious and I fear my students suffered as a result.' However, this can be taken as a witty admission of early career idealism rather than a statement of the approach that constituted her life's work. What this memoir makes crystal clear is that Olive championed a particular model of psycho-dynamically informed social work practice, and this book is worth reading alone for Olive's critical reflections on the nature of psycho-dynamic social work in Britain and the direction it and social work in general have taken since the 1970s. In this respect the memoir provides important revisionist insights.

These issues take on real importance in the context of perhaps the most important change to social work in Olive's lifetime. In her research into frontline practice in the mid-1970s she noted the 'wide ranging freedom which social workers had to choose the style and content of their direct work with clients' (Parsloe & Stevenson, 1978, p.134). The apparent discretion that workers had to shape their own practice has been heavily eroded today, as a shift has occurred from a psycho-dynamically informed model of social casework to an approach where practice has become much more regulated by managers and audit. It has become more about assessment, case management and signposting the service user to resources, as opposed to the worker herself and their relationship with the service-user being the resource and providing a long-term therapeutic service. Olive expresses some regret in this book that she didn't do more to defend psycho-dynamically informed social work from the attacks made on it or to more actively go further in developing a distinctly British psychodynamic theory-practice model. While the authenticity of her own feelings of disappointment and the integrity of her assessment of her role in the past must of course be respected, in my view she underplays in this memoir what she did achieve.

In fact, Olive mounted a robust defence of psycho-dynamic social casework when it came under attack in the 1950s and 1960s for being too influenced by psychoanalysis and making what were regarded as grandiose claims for how it could change people's psyches and behaviour. Barbara Wooton (1959) famously claimed that social workers were foolishly and ineptly attempting to be 'miniature psychoanalysts'. Olive responded to Wooton's criticisms in a wonderful article called 'The Understanding Caseworker', written a full fifty years ago (Stevenson, 1963), which still has a deep relevance to social work today.

In the article Olive gives a wonderful account of practice that went on in a car with ten-year-old Anne. Her foster placement, where she had lived for seven years, had broken down and the social worker – at that time known as a child care officer – was taking her to a residential care placement. Olive writes about how on the car journey Anne began to cry and wrapped herself in the worker's travel rug which she – Anne – referred to as her 'magic rug'. Safely wrapped in the rug and skilfully facilitated by the social worker to open up, the child talked about her very mixed feelings towards her foster family, her grief, anger, fears about the move, and her fantasies about going to a lovely new family home with nice children and adults. At lunch, the social worker talked to her about what the children's home looked like, the names of the people there and the children who would be in her group. With the travelling rug wrapped around her shoulders and clutching a teddy bear, the social worker's case record recorded how Anne then 'pretended to go to sleep, but obviously didn't and while she had her eyes shut managed to arrange herself across the seat so that her head was on my lap'. During the deep discussion about her feelings, Anne eventually got up and 'asked if she could have a jelly baby and took one out of the box on the car shelf' (p.93).

Olive writes of this piece of work:

> It is very clear in this record that the child care officer is not a 'miniature psychoanalyst' for her concern is not to explore deeply unconscious fantasy – which she is neither trained nor employed to do – but rather to recognize, as it were, the little pieces of the iceberg which show above the surface in order to help the child handle better the realities of the situation. On this long car journey, the child care officer is deliberately bridging the gap between the past and the future by the purposive references to both. The child care officer knows that in children who move from one place to another the images of people and places are often blurred and disturbed by the feelings – of anger, of fear, of sadness, which surround them, and that these are often intense. The task is therefore to try to keep the reality of the situation alive and relatively unclouded by fantasies. In order

to do this, the child care officer must be alive to the significance of
casual remarks or significant stories, such as Anne could tell when
encouraged by the magic rug and the child care officer's interest.

(Stevenson, 1963, p.95)

This superb articulation of what today we would call 'psycho-social'
theory and practice, exemplifies how those practitioners and
academics who shaped British social work in the 1960s and 1970s
– like Olive, Clare Winnicott (1963) and Juliet Berry (1972) – were
wise enough to understand that effective social work was only
concerned in very selective ways with the unconscious. Were any
attention to be given to the fantasy life of the client, crucially this
needed always to be in the context of their relationship to external
reality. In child care work it was experiences such as a move to a new
placement that brought the external reality of children having no
family home into sharp focus for these children, while also having a
deep impact on their emotional life. Best practice involved engaging
with both the internal and external aspects of children's and adult's
experiences (Kanter, 2004).

Olive argues that the ways in which the influence of psychoanalysis
on social work and child care in Britain has mostly been written
about is a caricature of what actually happened. The image has
grown up – or been promoted – of a generation of practitioners
whose main preoccupation was to delve into their client's
unconscious and explore their fantasy lives while ignoring their
social circumstances of poverty and discrimination. Just as in
classical psychoanalysis Freud interviewed people on the couch and
was preoccupied with their relationships with their mother and
father and their sexual and other fantasies, the story goes that the
social worker's focus was exclusively on their service user's internal
lives to the exclusion of the external factors that influenced their
experiences and life chances. It was this kind of alleged narrow
focus on the individual and their internal life and the practice of
social casework that the 'radical social work' movement began to
ferociously challenge in the mid-1970s (Bailey & Brake, 1975).
However, Olive points out that there were important differences
between the impact of psychoanalysis on American and British

social work. Psychoanalytically informed British social workers did not see their clients on the real or metaphorical couch, but were much more likely to work with them, as we have seen, in places like the service user's home and the social worker's car.

Olive acknowledges in this memoir that social work education in the 1950s and 1960s gave limited attention to social, economic and political factors. But she made efforts to make up for this by embracing the work of political philosophers like Paul Tillich (1960) on justice and she describes herself as always open and sometimes longing to learn more from sociology. This intellectual dilemma and practical question of how to integrate 'external' sociological factors and the individual and their 'internal' life – the classic problem of structure and agency – has always been a key theme in Olive's work. Here she is writing on 'Reflections on social work practice' in her 1989 edited collection *Child Abuse: Public Policy and Professional Practice*:

> We cannot afford (and neither can the children and families) to sustain theoretical dichotomies which have been so marked in the past 20 years. ... Some of these differences seem esoteric to practitioners, and the general indifference of British social workers to psychodynamic or behavioural theories means that there has been little debate among them, comparable to that sparked off by sociological and political theorists concerning poverty or by feminists. There is a pressing need for these issues to be re-addressed in education and training. Specifically, social workers need first to consider the utility in child-protection work of frameworks for understanding the micro-dynamics of family life and, secondly, the extent to which these can be integrated or reconciled with the analysis of wider forces in society which effect their clients.
>
> (Stevenson, 1989, pp.162–63)

In the same essay Olive notes that 'Ever since the late Barbara Wootton's blistering attack (1959) on social workers' use of psychodynamic theory, which coincided with increased awareness of post-welfare state poverty and increased sociological influences on social work, social workers have been extremely nervous of utilising such theory' (p.159). The negative view of psycho-dynamic social work as too concerned to 'pathologise' service users while ignoring their poverty and social exclusion had firmly taken hold. Olive is rightly scornful of the consequences of this repudiation of the self, emotions and the inner life of the child and worker, resulting in the absurdity of social work training producing child protection workers who allegedly do not know how to communicate with children. Olive seems to take a lot of responsibility for this state of affairs by writing self-critically in this book that she 'took her eye off the ball' by not defending and seeking to do more to develop psycho-dynamic social work. But one wonders what more she might have done? She provided a penetrating analysis of the theoretical and practice problems and she was innovative in trying to forge a new paradigm in which deeper understandings of the self and the social in interaction with one another can prevail. She communicated these messages through her writings, teaching and public lectures. Moreover, she led changes at the University of Nottingham in the late 1980s that sought to ensure students learned about how to work with children by introducing a 'nursery' placement for all students intending to work in social services departments (Stevenson, 1989, p.170).

In the memoir and in her brilliant paper about the work of Clare Winnicott (see Appendix I) Olive is doubtful about whether the skills deficit in direct work with children has changed much today. She passionately argues for the need for social work policy, education and practice to place centre-stage the capacity for skillful communication with children.

It could be easy to miss Olive's contribution as a theorist given that what she did not do was write purely theoretical papers or books in which she defended or developed psycho-dynamic approaches. While she did reflect to an extent on purely theoretical matters, notably in a contribution in 2005, the psycho-dynamic theories and ideas while ever present were always applied to real live social problems and the dynamics of interventions (Stevenson, 2005). Ultimately what she engaged in was applied psychoanalytic work in which the theory was deeply embedded in her analysis of the actual issues under consideration.

If anything, our debt to Olive is set to increase in the coming years as psycho-dynamic understandings of social work are making a comeback. The language today is different, but the broad intent similar, as notions such as 'relationship based practice', 'reflective practice' and 'reflective supervision' are now part of the mainstream. This is in recognition of the fact that emotions are central to practice and that there is a need to dislodge the excessive proceduralisation, 'tick-box' approaches and micro-management of practice referred to earlier. Concepts that Olive was writing about in the early 1960s, like Bion's theory of 'containment' (Stevenson, 1963), are regaining currency in social work today (Ruch, 2007).These theoretical developments are categorically not about focusing on the individual or the 'psyche' in isolation. This is a 'psycho-social' perspective which explores the interconnections between the sociological and the personal, internal and external, and how they interact in the minds and lives of service users and professionals (Froggett, 2002; Cooper & Lousada, 2005). There is also renewed interest in strands of theoretical inquiry that Olive opened up around social work on the move, in cars, on foot and on home visits (Ferguson, 2011). Olive, typically, played a very visible part in at least one strand of this renewal of psycho-dynamic thought through her involvement in the Centre for Social Work Practice, which hosts seminars and other initiatives that promote 'relationship based practice' in social work (www.cfswp.org). Olive was a constant presence at Centre for Social Work Practice events. According to one of the Centre leads, Andrew Cooper, Professor of Social Work at the Tavistock Clinic:

> Olive Stevenson has been an inspiration to several generations of social workers with a real concern to link children and families' developmental and relational struggles to the real world of child welfare and child protection policy and practice. Her thinking has always been rooted in the best traditions of applied psychoanalytic work, especially that of Clare Winnicott. She represents a tradition of genuine radicalism in this respect, a world view that recognises how poverty, inequality and the transmission of parenting patterns down the generations all intersect, and must be engaged with in the round by practitioners and policy makers.

In this memoir Olive has remained true to her convictions as an applied psychoanalytic scholar, providing an intimate portrait of herself as a complex individual whose life has been shaped by a range of internal and external forces. She writes for instance of the challenges of being a lesbian, especially at a time when it was, as she puts it, socially denied and how she sublimated any desire to have children and 'channelled powerful maternal feelings' into her work. And she is open about how she has had to struggle with destructive feelings such as envy in competitive environments like universities. It is a redemptive book in how it shows that it is through moral courage and becoming conscious of such emotions (through therapy and good professional supervision) that one can hope to live with and handle internal conflicts and become a better, loving person and professional as a result.

In the course of thinking about and writing these introductory remarks and talking to others about Olive, people have shared many memories and spoken with great warmth and appreciation for her and her work. This was my experience of her too. Having admired her from afar for many years I only got to actually meet and talk with her for the first time in 2003, at a conference. It was the first of many exchanges I have been fortunate enough to have with Olive in which she generously shared her knowledge and supported my work. Her academic brilliance and humanity attracted people to her and stories are common of how people would want to be around her and wait in the wings of conferences and other public events. Some would want to talk, others would simply want to be able to touch her. She would joke that she needed to give time for her 'hem to be kissed'. This memoir can ensure that future generations in social work will go on being able to touch the wisdom, insight and genius of Olive Stevenson.

Harry Ferguson
Professor of Social Work
Centre for Social Work
University of Nottingham
2013

References

Bailey R. & Brake M. (1975), *Radical Social Work*, Edward Arnold: London.

Berry J. (1972), *Social Work with Children,* Routledge & Kegan Paul: London.

Becker S., Aldridge J. & Dearden C. (1988), *Young Carers and their Families*, Blackwell Science: Oxford.

Butler I. & Drakeford M. (2011), *Social Work on Trial: The Maria Colwell Case and the State of Welfare*, Policy Press: Bristol.

Cooper A. & Lousada J. (2005), *Borderline Welfare: Feeling and Fear of Feeling in Modern Welfare*, Karnac: London.

Department of Health and Social Security (1974), *Report of the Committee of Inquiry into the Care and Supervision Provided in Relation to Maria Colwell*, HMSO: London.

Ferguson H. (2011), *Child Protection Practice*, Palgrave Macmillan: Basingstoke.

Froggett L. (2002), *Love, Hate and Welfare: Psychosocial approaches to policy and practice*, Policy Press: Bristol.

Hallett C. & Stevenson O. (1980), *Child Abuse: Aspects of Inter-professional Communication*, Allen & Unwin: London.

Jones K. (1984), *Eileen Younghusband: A Biography*, Bedford Square Press: London.

Kanter J. (2004), *Face to Face with Children: The Life and Work of Clare Winnicott*, Karnac Books: London.

Niechcial J. (2010), *Lucy Faithful, Mother to Hundreds*, self-published, available from jfmniechal@hotmail.com.

Parton N. (2004), 'From Maria Colwell to Victoria Climbié: reflections on public inquiries into child abuse a generation apart', *Child Abuse Review*, 13(2) pp.80–94.

Ruch G. (2007), 'Reflective practice in contemporary child care social work: The role of containment', *British Journal of Social Work*, 37(4) pp.659–80.

Stevenson O. (1954), 'The First Treasured Possession: A study of the part played by specially loved objects and toys in the lives of certain children', *Psychoanalytic Study of the Child*, 9.

Stevenson O. (1963), 'The Understanding Caseworker', *New Society*, 1 August. Reprinted in Holgate E. (ed.) (1972) *Communicating with Children*, Longman: London.

Stevenson O. (1971), Editorial, *British Journal of Social Work*, 1(1) 1–3.

Stevenson O. (ed.) (1989), *Child Abuse: Professional Practice and Public Policy*, Harvester Wheatsheaf: London.

Stevenson O. (2005), 'Foreword' in Bower M. (ed.), *Psychoanalytic Theory for Social Work Practice: Thinking Under Fire*, Routledge: London.

Tillich P. (1960), *Love, Power and Justice*, Oxford University Press: New York.

Winnicott C. (1963), *Child Care and Social Work*, Bookstall Publications.

Winnicott D. (1951), 'Transitional objects and transitional phenomena', *International Journal of Psycho-Analysis*, 34, pp.89–97.

Winnicott D. (1971), *Playing and Reality*, Routledge: London.

Wittenberg-Salzberger I. (1970), *Psychoanalytic Insight and relationships: A Kleinian Approach*, Routledge & Kegan Paul: London.

Wooton B. (1959), *Social Science and Social Pathology*, Allen & Unwin: London.

Introduction

It is important to me to try and understand some of the factors in my experience and personality which played a part in the choice of career and in the way I have seen the role of social work (and, in my case, as a social work educator). To be an effective social worker, there has to be a dynamic interplay between emotion and intellect. This has to happen if one is to use oneself effectively in the service of others.

In my case, I am clear that my choice of career was no accident. How far this is true for others I cannot say. Many have told me that 'it just happened, I saw an advertisement', or some such. (I always wonder however, how many other advertisements did not take their eye.) The earliest indication that something was brewing was at my interview with the headmistress of Whitgift Grammar School, Croydon when I told her that I wanted to do psychology when I grew up. She later wrote to my mother suggesting that I should not read Freud yet. Of course, I had no idea what psychology was. But as I look back on those early years, I see three characteristics which, put together, seem like a foundation for future interest in social work.

First, I was immensely curious, some would say nosey, as a little child. I listened avidly to, sometimes whispered, adult conversations; keen to find out about the family (mostly in Ireland) and vastly intrigued by stories about the neighbours. As I write this, my head is full of pictures of the neighbours. By the time I was seven (1937) and the Second World War was looming, I was preoccupied with the stories of the single women, some sisters, in my road: the Misses Read, Misses Pettigate and Miss Marjorie Reeves. All looked after mothers with ambivalent devotion, some of them had 'little jobs' such as in Boots' lending library. All had experienced sad losses in the First World War. Shellshock was a familiar and frightening word. Tales of being gassed in the trenches made a particular impact – it was my only real fear when 'our' war broke out and we were issued with gas masks.

Second, I soaked up other people's feelings, especially I think, their anxieties. My parents had a great deal to be anxious about, as I will explain further. To this day, I find intense anxiety in others hard to bear. Left to myself, I am not a very anxious person. In general, I am keenly aware of how others may be feeling whether or not I cope with it well. Again, this is essential in a social work role.

The third reason (though this has taken a long time to face) was that I now realise that my parents' difficulty in expressing anger towards others, or even disagreement between themselves, left me with a profound sense of unease about the expression of these negative emotions in myself, and a longing for processes of mediation and reconciliation. In complex ways, this desire for reconciliation explains the intellectual energy which I have expended on making links between ideas or professions which are sometimes polarised or far apart. This has offered me some of my richest professional and academic opportunities: for example, as a social work teacher, the extent to which I could bring together different theories of human behaviour for the better understanding of the person to be helped; or the development of 'inter-professional working' in child protection.

So this memoir is a particular kind of journey, which tries to describe the making of a social worker from childhood. The journey passes through some very dark places, in my private life and working life (which cannot be separated) and it does not lead to a comfortable resting place.

The decision to allow my personal life a degree of publicity has raised ethical issues, some of which affect the narrative. A story which brings to life a particular episode is good to read and often conveys more than an abstract, condensed comment. Yet it may identify or hurt other people who had no expectation of being included. For this reason, I have been restrained.

1

Early Years & Influences

Family Life

Early memories are episodic; snapshots with little context. So the facts of this story have been pieced together by me and other friends and family members, facts coloured by personal feelings. But there is a good deal which is solid.

I am told that about 7am on a December morning, my mother said, 'I think I'll be going now John', and walked with him to the nearby nursing home in South Croydon where I was born. It was 13 December 1930. This spare account is all I have. In later years, when I asked if it had hurt, my mother replied, 'Yes, but you soon forget about it because you want the baby'. There were telegrams announcing my birth; my paternal grandmother, when told my name was Olive, sent a telegram by return asking, 'Why not Olivia?' I was 6lbs 8oz and healthy. My brother Kenneth was, at that time, six years old and my half-sister, Marjorie, 18.

My parents and sister, Marjorie had come to England from Dublin in 1920. My father, John, was a civil servant in the Irish government before independence. He left when Ireland became a Republic, fearing religious discrimination in his career if he stayed. He was a Protestant and 'The Troubles' in the years preceding 1922 gave him good reason to feel insecure about his future. He was the eldest of a very large, poor family and had struggled, through evening classes, to get on the civil service ladder to a secure career.

None of his brothers and sisters achieved much educationally, some being in that dreaded category of 'ne'er do well'. There was a strong whiff of disapproval in my parents' attitudes towards them. My father was, I believe, frightened lest they should turn to him for money. My mother saw in them a flamboyance, a 'dodginess' which she disliked. I have wondered whether she feared that I had inherited a tendency to show off. Showing off was a cardinal sin in her family. Tales of the naughty aunts in my father's family filtered through. Did one of them really run up an unpaid account for fur coats at *Switzers*, Dublin's posh shop? Should we take it seriously that she was struck on the head by a brick when she was 18 and was 'never the same again'? And what about the one who went to Canada and launched herself into an evangelical career with her newly founded sect, The Church of God? And could she *really* have hired the Royal Albert Hall for a rally? What was I to make of the aunt who visited us in wartime in ATS uniform and told me that I mustn't mind when she passed me in the street, she would be on secret business. Thrilled, I ran to tell my mother, standing at the cooker. I think I can hear the sniff of disbelief and disapproval. My father's brothers were less sensational but still 'not quite'. Only one of his siblings, Violet, established herself as a person warmly welcomed into the family.

As I write this, I feel the struggle between a legitimate perception of people it was reasonable to avoid and the discomfort of class prejudice. My mother's family had a phrase, 'a cut above buttermilk' to describe those who had escaped the label of 'working class'. All through my childhood, I was told that my paternal grandfather (who was a tiny man) was a 'masseur'. I was puzzled but I accepted this. In my later years, long after my mother had died, her sister told me, in a burst of candour, that he had been a public baths attendant.

When we watch costume drama on television, we see played out the world in which the social hierarchy affects relationships blatantly and cruelly. Unsurprisingly, in the early days of sociology as an academic discipline, the issue of social class was central to the development of one's identity. The extent to which all this affected my attitudes is embarrassingly illustrated by a vivid memory from when I was about ten or eleven. Reading the newspaper on the floor, I looked up at my mother and asked; 'Mum, what social class are we? Upper-middle class?' A silence: then reluctantly but honestly, 'No dear, lower, I think.'

The significance given to social class in the attitudes and accounts on the maternal side of the family was very strong. It affected not only the way in which my father's family was viewed but also the members of their own family. Essentially, this approach came from my maternal grandmother whose father had been a middle-class Englishman with some pretentions to social status and an 'agreeable tenor voice' but who (we lower the voice) was not reliable. He had four sons and a daughter; my grandmother, Caroline (Carrie) Shepherd was the youngest child.

I was told of my grandmother's anger at having to act as a 'skivvy' to the boys in her family, even having to clean their shoes. This, I was told, caused her to flee into a marriage when she was only seventeen years old. That she only had daughters in her marriage makes one wonder about the power of mind over matter. There was no doubt that she had educational aspirations for her daughters; she herself, I was told, played the piano and spoke French. She married Richard Dobbs, a solicitor's clerk, from a farming family. He lacked the ambition or refinement of his wife, although the pencil stub in his waistcoat, with which he did the *Irish Times* crossword, suggests hidden depths. The picture is of a disappointed wife who is somehow felt to have 'married beneath her' but a darker and sadder side of their marriage (only acknowledged to me when I was adult) was that in the early years of the marriage, when the girls were young, my grandfather drank and gambled away his wages, all spent on the evening after payday. He would often return home with a present for Carrie, such as a pair of gloves, when they needed food. My grandmother took to going on payday to the firm where he worked to intercept the wages. The humiliation felt would have been huge for a woman for whom respectability was so important.

Their four daughters were born at two-year intervals; Lily, Evelyn (my mother), May and Hilda. There was one more child who died at birth, Olive. Have I made this connection for myself or was I really told that when I was born (the first female child of the sisters) I was regarded as a replacement for the fifth sibling? It is the maternal side of the family which dominated my childhood.

My father had been married before. This was little spoken of but the sadness of it was implicit in the reticence. His wife had died of tuberculosis (TB) at the age of 23, having had several miscarriages before that. The surviving child, Marjorie, had been cared for by her grandparents who had offered to keep her when my parents decided to move to England. My mother told me very firmly that she had said to my father, 'Her place is with us'. Thus, this little girl joined them in London and was 18 years old when I was born. It was about then that she was diagnosed with TB as her mother had been. She had been interviewed for a job and it was discovered at the medical. There were no antibiotics in 1930. These are the facts, pieced together by a curious child living in an emotional climate which was powerfully controlled in front of the children.

What is crystal clear, however, is that the first five years of my life were clouded by ever-present worry, tension and fear about Marjorie's health. These were the days before the NHS; my father was on the modest salary of an Executive Officer in the Civil Service. Fees for medical care, including nursing homes, must have been a nightmare. In the year after my birth, I am told, I cried incessantly. Doctors were called in and could find nothing wrong. My brother (most rare this) told me in later years that he had found my mother crying and saying that she did not have enough milk to feed me. This was the year that Marjorie became ill. Later, when I began to have heavy colds, the doctor advised my mother not to dress me in over-warm clothes.

My struggle to understand family events is well illustrated by one vivid memory I have of Marjorie. That is of Christmas Day, 1935; I was five and she was 23. My mother took me to see her in a nursing home on Christmas morning; I took her a potted plant. She was sitting up in bed looking cheerful. Flash forward a few hours. I am sitting in my Aunt Hilda's dining room, on the floor, playing bagatelle. My father comes into the room, puts his gloves on the table and says, 'It's all over'. I didn't know what was all over but I did not ask. Thereafter there is a gap. My next memory is of going upstairs to where my mother is cleaning and saying, 'What's happened to Marjorie?' My mother answers, 'She has passed away'. But I did not know what that meant. I went into the garden and asked my father, 'What does "passed away" mean?' My father tells me that it means 'died' but does not ask me why I ask.

I have no memory of anything to do with the funeral which was held at a local church. I think my parents were part of a generation which rejected the Victorian indulgence of grief. My aunt told me how horrified she had been as a child to be shown the dead in open coffins. That generation were also involved in the First World War in which bereavement and loss were on a scale so appalling that emotional restraint was necessary for survival. (Although they were of course Irish, my father had been in the British Army.)

I believe that the keeping of anything unpleasant, especially death, away from me was well intentioned. However, my parents were also dealing with their own anxiety and depression. How far these were personality traits, how far they arose from sad events and circumstances is impossible for me to know.

Certainly, there would have been fear of infection, especially for me as an infant. As a small child I was prone to heavy colds; my icy bedroom was warmed with coal fires – a sure sign of illness – and my father brought home grapes and a peach from the market. (I loved the feel of the peach skin in my hands.) When I was five – after Marjorie had died – I could not begin school because I had whooping cough so badly. I was sent to Ireland with my mother to convalesce. I remember the beef tea made in the range by Granny, the rooks cawing down the chimney in my bedroom, my insistence on covering my bed with towels in case I was sick when I coughed and my delight on waking up to a clean bed.

As with so many things, I wish I could now tell my parents that I have some inkling as to how awful it must have been for them to hear me 'coughing my lungs up' so soon after Marjorie's death. And to convey to my father my pain for his pain in watching Marjorie die just as his first wife had done.

As I write this, the people whom I believe loved me in those early years walk through my mind: my mother and father; my brother, six years older and very protective; Marjorie who my mother said was very fond of me (it is part of a precious memory that she smiled at me lovingly when I took her that plant on Christmas Day). In this circle too was my aunt Hilda. She had come from Dublin to study singing at the Royal College of Music and lived with us throughout that time until she married when I was four.

My family did their best to protect me as well as they could. But an intelligent, demanding, curious and sensitive child cannot be protected against certain events and the powerful emotions which were in the very daily stuff of our family life, dominated by anxiety and fear.

Religion

To be a child of Southern Irish Protestants over the last eighty years, even though I was brought up in England, is to ensure some deeply rooted feelings centred upon religious issues and intertwined socio-political factors.

My parents' background, as far as I am aware, was staunchly Protestant and with that came political affiliations with the United Kingdom. My father (who had emigrated to England in 1920 when the Irish Free State was formed) and mother struggled with their attitudes and feelings about Roman Catholicism; at best, there was ambivalence, at worst dislike and distrust. Once away from Ireland, they sought to achieve tolerance; my mother used to ask me, of friends coming to tea, 'Tell me, dear, is she a Protestant? Not that it makes any difference'.

While my father, who held (at least more openly) less tolerant views, influenced me through the passion as well as the content of his views about Roman Catholic doctrine. In naughtier moments, much disapproved of by mother, he would sing anti-Catholic words to the tune of 'Lily Bolero'.

Before I was nine, I had asked about the meaning of terms like 'transubstantiation' and reacted with disgust to the Catholic idea of

Holy Communion: bread turning into flesh, wine into blood. What? My father, his nose twitching with emotion, spoke of the wickedness of the concept of original sin which resulted in the rush to baptism of dying children. Less obviously, but hugely significant to me, was the looming power of the Catholic Church in Southern Ireland. My grandfather referred to trainee priests, who processed along the roads of Greystones (near Dublin) as 'crows'.

Yet this picture, which may seem one of unalloyed bigotry, was not the whole story. Recognition, at least, of the need for tolerance, led my parents to control and moderate these views. Later, my mother and her sisters sought and found a much loved cousin who had been cast out when he married a Catholic. There was great rejoicing. However, neither of my parents identified with any branch of the Protestant Church once in England. They raised no objection to my joining the Congregational Church at which my aunt was a choir leader, but I was always aware that they could not enter into this aspect of my life. Indeed, my father told quite bitter stories of excessive Sunday churchgoing in his childhood and of hell-fire preaching. Although the word was never used, I suspect they would have considered themselves agnostics. My father may also have been influenced by the tragic death of his first wife.

It is impossible to disentangle personal characteristics and education from the underlying influences of my parents. How did this all affect my attitude toward religion? I can see important threads. First, even as an outsider and an agnostic, I am not indifferent to religious issues. I am affected emotionally by what happens within and between religious groups.

Second, despite this enduring interest, I have never had any kind of emotional experience in which my faith transcended the need for 'proof'.

Third, my distrust of the Catholic Church has in fact increased over the years, though there was a long period of pseudo-tolerance. In my adult years, much has come to light about the physical and sexual abuse of children in Ireland. But more generally, I abhor the power which the Irish Catholic Church held over its populace, epitomised in attitudes to sexuality. Comparatively recently, I heard of the gynaecological operations carried out, as late as the 1950s, in Dublin to avoid women having caesareans which might have limited future childbirth. These involved, on some occasions, the breaking of the pelvis and rendered some women permanently disabled.

However, my scepticism extends beyond Catholicism. As I engaged with the Congregational Church in my teens, I found myself on a coach trip to Haringey to hear the popular American evangelist, Billy Graham. The stadium was packed. In the Bible reading, I recall, Herod asks Salome to bring him the head of John the Baptist on a platter. After the reading, we were asked to go to the front if we had 'heard the call'. I watched with astonishment as people formed queues to be saved and felt socially excluded. What was this all about?

This uneasiness was epitomised by my ambivalent decision to be 'received' into the Congregational Church, the non-conformist equivalent to confirmation. I had decided to do this in my teens when I was busily engaged in the church youth group, but I can still recall the sense of guilt and unease when the moment came to receive the bread and wine, even though I knew it was regarded by Congregationalists as only symbolic of the body and blood of Christ.

Over the years I have engaged with, in a detached but comfortable way, the beautiful works and music of the Anglican Church. Now, even as I write, we are in the midst of a nonsensical (or so it seems) and bitter dispute, maybe schism, still focussing on sexuality, which appears to be the dominant preoccupation of the church.

So where does all this leave me now, in my old age? I am sure that I will die an agnostic. I do not presume to be an atheist. Too many people whom I respect, both intellectually and personally, have held religious convictions for me to deny them any validity. I dislike the self-righteous tone of the Richard Dawkins critique.

I am also left with a deep fear and dislike of dogmatism, which has characterised so much religious debate from the Catholic-Protestant schism to our present preoccupation with Islam. The Irish story, including the last years of the troubles in Northern

Ireland, shows what can be unleashed. There is an uncomfortable side to this; many God-fearing Protestants in Northern Ireland had no truck with the violence, or, of course, its associated criminality. But their obdurate attitudes have provided a granite wall against which negotiations have been smashed, time and time again.

For many years, I have respected the ways in which the Quakers express their faith. In the 1960s when I was still working out a way of living as a lesbian, I read their pamphlet, 'Towards a Quaker view of sex' in which the issue of gay and lesbian sexuality was specifically addressed. I remember a great sense of relief at the liberal views expressed, at a time when this was far from the norm.

In more recent years, my long-standing friend Phyllida Parsloe has become a Quaker and everything I hear confirms my earlier respect. But, even given their moral and theological flexibility, I have no inclination to join up.

I am grateful for the framework of morality which Christianity has given me; at least for the 'pick & mix' that I have chosen. I am sure that Humanists will point out that morality does not have to derive from Christianity – indeed, most great religions at their root espouse similar values. But there is a sense of rootedness, of belonging to a long tradition which came home to me very powerfully when I first visited Jerusalem in the 1970s, the first of many academic exchanges. Surely, the current distasteful and rather stupid battles over sexuality will seem trivial and irrelevant as the years pass? But at the core of morality, which is about treating others as you would yourself like to be treated, is its capacity of indefinite extension to individuals and social situations, the right basis for social work.

2

Reflections on Health & Healthcare

Born in 1930, my childhood and teens were lived before the creation of the National Health Service (NHS). I have no recollection of my parents ever talking directly about medical expenses. But I know from oblique comments that my early years were spent in an atmosphere of intense anxiety about the health of my half- sister, Marjorie who was diagnosed with tuberculosis at eighteen. After her diagnosis there were five years of expense on nursing homes and sanatoria, although fashionable Switzerland could not, of course, be afforded. Even without that particular experience, it would not have been long before I absorbed the prevailing fear of TB, especially amongst Irish immigrants. As discussed earlier, my father's first wife, Marjorie's mother, had died of this. I was born into this pervading sense of sadness and worrying. When I got whooping cough very badly my mother and I were shipped off to Ireland to my grandparents for convalescence. It is hard to imagine the impact all this had on my poor parents. Just after the death of one, another child seems to be coughing herself to death in turn. All this, of course, is before vaccination or antibiotics.

Into these early years came my Uncle Gerald, my Aunt Hilda's husband. Uncle Geb, as I called him, was a local general practitioner (GP) and anaesthetist at the cottage hospital. He was a good deal older than my aunt and a committed Christian. My aunt met him through the Congregational Church. He was a single-handed practitioner, not so unusual in those days. In the period before the NHS, he looked after all of us without charge and I know that my parents deeply appreciated this.

Uncle Geb, I can now see, has been influential in a variety of ways and on different levels, in my understanding and attitudes to health services and healthcare generally. Like my father (and more so), my uncle was a bitter opponent of socialism and saw the introduction of the NHS as a disaster. Yet, like my father, his formal position on politics bore no relation to his behaviour towards those who needed his help. Accepting that there is a process of idealisation here, it seems certain from what I have been told, that he was a much loved and respected GP in his community. As he grew older, my aunt worried about the strain of his workload which included his regular late night visit to help a woman whose mother would not go to bed until he arrived. The surgery was in the family house and, twice a day, which began with my aunt's 7.30am polishing of the brass plate on the gate and ended at midnight when my uncle finished his paperwork, the household was geared to the service of patients. As I progressed through childhood ailments and was visited at home, I recall the feeling of safety when, in the bitterly cold bedrooms of pre-war years, he warmed his large capable hands at the gas fire before he examined me. Later, when I had my appendix out, he was the anaesthetist and I remember vividly how content I felt as he told me to count to ten before I faded away.

Uncle Geb (whom I nicknamed 'Jelly Roll' after the jazz musician Jelly Roll Morton) was in many ways a kind of symbol of the GP we long for and very rarely experience. It seems to me that much of the persistent discontent about medical care, in spite of hugely improved resources, reflects the longing to be cared for when we are unwell and to trust in the good intentions of those who look after us. Without that basic level of faith in the encounter, there is no security upon which to build when anxiety is high. Over the years, I have observed how one's sensibilities and sensitivities are heightened at times of such stress; so for example, I remember visits to Accident & Emergency more in relation to how I was treated as a person than what was 'done to me'. I recall, when having a bad cut on my head stitched that it surprised and helped me when the nurse held my hand.

As the NHS becomes the focus of more and more media attention, I find myself reluctant to face the revelations of insensitive and unkind care, especially in the nursing of older people. I am still shocked to the roots of my being when I read of older people who are given no help to eat, or who soil themselves when having to wait too long.

Let me be clear; I am not suggesting that things are not what they used to be. The picture both of past and present is extremely complex. But the impact of my Uncle Geb has been profound in giving me a powerful internalised image of the essential ingredients of professional love in patient care.

Despite the early years of chest-related complaints, I went into the latency years and adolescence as a healthy girl. My self-image was of a robust person, with little or no time off school or, later, while at university or work. There were underlying emotional worries associated with my family, but these did not take somatic (physical) forms in my formative years, except for some problems concerned with sleeping.

Long shadows of illness were, however, thrown across my path as I grew up, relating most of all to my mother's family and bowel cancer. As my brother married, on a cold January day in 1944, my mother was grief-stricken by the news that her mother was dying in Ireland. The day was darkened whilst we all pretended all was well. Then, in the 1960s, my mother was diagnosed with the same cancer and survived surgery, only to die from secondaries in the liver not long afterwards. Again, bleak memories of her last few weeks when she was cared for by my aunt. In the 1980s, the eldest of my mother's sisters died, again from bowel cancer, and my Aunt Hilda survived surgery for the same condition in the 1990s.

This rather worrying history of bowel cancer on the maternal side led me to seek genetic advice and regular colonoscopies were advised, thankfully all of which proved negative. But, somehow, so far as I am aware, this has not been a profound conscious anxiety.

These women; my grandmother and three of her daughters, presented a picture so different from my own that I did not identify with their bodies (though I did in many other ways). They were, as were so many of their generation, martyrs to constipation; cups without handles used to soak senna pods were a feature of the larder and there was much talk of the usefulness of stewed prunes. Their diet was light years away from my own, which follows current trends, as I obsessively consume fruit and vegetables.

Looking back, I see the first signs that my body and my emotions may have been interacting unhelpfully with a mystery illness in the early 1980s when I became deeply fatigued and, for the first and only time in my career, was signed off sick for the best part of a term. It is temptingly easy, with hindsight, to talk of chronic fatigue syndrome, much less well understood at that time. Equally, I had been on the pill (for medical reasons) for a number of years and the 'collapse' occurred when the doctors recommended that I should stop the pill and did not for some time prescribe hormone replacement therapy (HRT).

At the time, and newly arrived at Keele University, I was the first woman Professor of Social Policy and Social Work to be appointed there and under considerable pressure. But I suspect that, if the soma was taking instruction from the psyche, it was as much to do with the guilt I felt at establishing a new relationship – and as I felt, betraying someone else – as it was the demands of the new job. However, the Keele community, which was close, gossipy and not benign, made the management of a lesbian relationship particularly difficult.

This period of illness was one from which I have learned a lot. It was my first experience as an adult of a degree of dependency where I had to rely on others for daily help. I came to understand how much the freedom to do ordinary things as and when you want can matter. People who kindly offer to shop may not buy the right kind of biscuits but you have to be grateful. I also remember with vivid clarity the feelings of exhaustion which made me struggle to walk a few hundred yards up the hill to attend my friend Phyllida Parsloe's inaugural lecture at Bristol (and this when I was getting better).

I also recall with embarrassment how proud I was to report that I had been able to clean some silver that morning. In the context of my work (I lived on campus), I have never resolved the feelings of guilt and anger which I felt when the person who had to act up as head of department expressed her resentment at what she described as 'my lack of commitment'.

I took away from this episode some awareness of the life-long tension between dependence and independence which can be raised by health issues and (though with less clarity) of the interaction of mind and body in a passionate and troubled person.

The early 1980s would prove to be the point when I had to take my health into account and I began to adjust to a new self-image which was not so robust as I thought it was. In 1984, I moved to Nottingham University. I had the first of what were to be annual mammograms, and a biopsy on my left breast. Nothing was found and although, at some level, it must have been worrying, I was not conscious of that to any extent. This spanned a period of further emotional upheaval and in 1988 and 1989 there began a series of investigations into what began as a major crop of mouth and tongue ulcers (made much worse by inflammation in the mouth). Over many months I saw a specialist, who tried a number of drugs, including thalidomide, which made me feel very unwell indeed. Eventually, although with some uncertainty, there was a diagnosis of Sjögren's Syndrome (a disease of the auto-immune system, akin to lupus, with symptoms of dry eyes and dry mouth) and decreasing doses of steroids were prescribed (which I still take, though very near the minimum daily dose). It is under control, much aided by eye drops and sugar-free chewing gum.

This diagnosis of a condition which is incurable, firmly established in my mind a degree of physical vulnerability which I had been reluctant to acknowledge. However, I see now that my close friends would have been more conscious of my physical limitations. They knew of my mammograms and colonoscopies, of my Sjögren's Syndrome, of my endless battles with upset bowels when I ate any (remotely) fatty food and, in earlier years, of powerfully adverse reactions to insect bites. These last two were a plague to them when we were on holiday, involving as they did visits to foreign doctors and hospitals. I must have been a pain to be with on holiday. Back home, I settled back into familiar food and climate and was little troubled.

3

Early Interest in Social Work

In previous chapters, I have tried to paint a picture of my early childhood and the ways in which it may have led to a choice of social work as a career. However, this choice was made possible by the creation of the Welfare State in post-war Britain. In 1948, the year before I went to university, the Children Act was passed, part of a huge raft of 'welfare' legislation. That Act laid the foundations for Children's Departments in local government and created a new branch of social work to be carried out by Child Care Officers; I joined in 1954. Even without that specific opportunity, it seems likely that I would have found a place somewhere in the emerging profession, divided into special areas of practice as it was until 1970.

A Children's Home in Croydon: First Experiences of Social Care

I wish I could remember what gave me the idea of working in a children's home when I left school, before university. Certainly, no one in the family knew about such matters. In 1948, at the age of seventeen, I began work as an assistant house mother in a small children's home run by the London borough of Croydon. The children's officer was Kenneth Brill (later to be my boss in Devon). He was one of a group of pioneers – in fact, mostly women – who were battling to develop children's services within local government.

My memories of that children's home in Croydon are still vivid. It was run by an ex-nurse, Miss Nash, or 'Matron'; a strict but not generally harsh woman. There was, however, one episode which has stayed with me: Eric, one of a group of brothers, refused food; I was later told to hold him down whilst Matron tried to feed him, at which point he promptly vomited. I have often wondered about the futility (borne, I believe, of anxiety) of that exercise. But, also, it made me aware of how *powerless* junior staff may feel in such a circumstance. That issue of power in residential care has stayed with me all my life and was the theme of a memorial lecture I gave for Quetta Rabley (a London County Council social worker). In that lecture, I argued that, for different reasons, all the parties in residential care may feel powerless and believe that power lies elsewhere.

It was at this home that I also began to observe children quite closely – though with no theory to draw upon. In particular, I worried about Freddie, who (I can now see clearly) was learning disabled. I saw him pulling insects to pieces with relish and being unkind to animals. So, how's this for chutzpah? I made an appointment to see Mr Brill and his deputy to tell him of my worries. (He listened but gave little away!)

An Undergraduate at Oxford

As soon as I reached Oxford University in 1949 where I had a place to read English Language and Literature, I was (pleasurably) bombarded with information about social and leisure activities. Amongst them was a society 'Come, a Challenge', which arranged visits, one of which was to the Mulberry Bush School at Standlake, run by Barbara Dockar-Drysdale (known as 'Mrs D') who was in the 'Winnicott Circle'. (More on Clare and Donald Winnicott later.) This was a school for so-called 'maladjusted' children; the buildings were ramshackle and the children were amongst the most emotionally disturbed and/or deprived in the country. My visit made a huge impression on me, particularly when Mrs D spoke to a child who shouted noisily through a window at us. She engaged with the child in a direct but courteous manner and I had the glimmerings of what therapeutic communication with children might be about.

This one visit convinced me to work at the Mulberry Bush for part of my first two long vacations. I absorbed a way of approaching children which was fundamental to my later work, as well as giving me a 'sense' of theory, though not in any systematic way. The psychoanalytic basis of the work, especially in relation to the Winnicotts, entered my understanding without conscious thought. In a sense it was a foundation for the later years of training at the London School of Economics (LSE) with Clare Winnicott as my tutor.

I became aware, during my second spell of work at the Mulberry Bush, that I was becoming uneasy in my working relationship with Barbara Dockar-Drysdale. I doubt if she was aware of it – we were in awe of her and I was an inexperienced, somewhat gauche young woman. Physical conditions at the school were at the time very poor, including hygiene (cats on the dining tables, for example) and I felt that this was rationalised away rather than regretted ('necessary for therapy'). So I experienced the very sharp edge of Mrs D's tongue if I raised anything which might have been thought of as critical. However, I recognise in those exchanges a recurring problem in my early career (and perhaps earlier still). I was greatly excited by the world I was learning about, and very articulate, but tactless in my questions. What those in authority over me probably did not realise is that I was easily crushed and made to feel foolish in these exchanges. At that stage, I had no sense of being a threat to such people.

My period at Oxford, reading English, fitted in very well with my career intentions. Although I was not a particularly clever student, I was fascinated by the dynamics and structure of drama and in general by the insight which literature throws on human relationships. Indeed, when I came to teach social work at Oxford in the 1960s, I initiated seminars for social work students using various forms of literature, including biography and novels. At this stage in the development of social work education, it was still possible to frame a curriculum with some flexibility. But, as the years went by, social work attempted 'genericism' and there was more general direction; such diversions could not be sustained.

4

Becoming a Social Worker

Postgraduate Studies at the London School of Economics (1952/1953)

Reaching the end of my undergraduate days, my plans for the future were clearly founded on the idea of some kind of social work. I toyed at the time with training for psychiatric social work in the United States (at that time quite adventurous). But then I heard of the LSE Child Care Course and of the need for a basic social science qualification first. Financial support was essential – my father had retired the year I went to Oxford. Thus, I presented myself for interview at the Home Office with Sybil Clement-Brown, then in charge of the developing training for Child Care Officers at a few university centres. I cannot recall why I thought that funding might be possible for both the years of postgraduate study, rather than just the professional second year. When I mentioned it, I was told firmly that it was not possible to fund the social science year. I suppose my disappointment was evident. Perhaps because the Home Office was anxious to build up a cadre of good graduates and my experience and interests were unusually, in one so young, focussed, it became possible – I have never understood how – to fund both years of my study.

So, in 1952, I arrive at the LSE, insisting on living in squalid digs in London, rather than in the comfort of my family home in suburban London. (However, I did take my washing home.) That first year of basic social science was of very variable quality or, at least, did not arouse my intellectual curiosity as had Oxford. Basic economics was incomprehensible and boring to me. Who was this 'Rational Man' whose decisions determined our economic behaviour? More seriously, I do not recall any sociology teaching, a deficit of which I became very aware when I later went back to teach in Professor Albert 'Chelly' Halsey's department in Oxford, at the time a hive of sociological activity. In the early days of my academic career, I spent much time trying to bring together in my head the contrasting, but not necessarily conflicting, perspectives from psychoanalytic theory and sociology and their application to social work.

The foundations of my interest in social policy and the place of social work within it were certainly laid at this stage. I still remember the fascination with which I read R.H. Tawney (1880–1962) and thought for the first time of the moral, political and social basis for the Welfare State, to which I enthusiastically belonged.

At this time, the basic social science course provided some field work experience, which included for me a spell at the Paddington Family Welfare Association (FWA) office. I was assigned the case of 'Percy', an elderly widower living in a damp basement flat. I cannot remember what I was supposed to do beyond 'supporting' him, but I flung myself into that task, inducing, as I now see, an inappropriate dependency in him – after all I was not going to be there for long. I remember telling him I would keep in touch and then feeling dreadful because I did not do so. Indeed a few years later, when I met my FWA supervisor and she told me Percy was still asking about me, I felt seriously guilty. I think that experience opened my head and heart to a different kind of social issue: the loneliness of many old people for whom family links no longer work and how best to help. There was no clear connection to my own experience at that time but – as so much in this period of my life – it laid the foundations for a career-long interest in matters concerning vulnerable elderly people. Although my subsequent training and early career focussed on children, it has been a very important strand in my work and contributed to an interest in the generic bases to social work.

There are also learning points which can only be a product of actual experience. I recall the visit to the FWA office of an elderly woman, who told me at great length of her persecution by the neighbours. It seemed that they had so organised their vacuum cleaning that they could poke through the floorboards of her flat and spy on her. Indignant, I rang the local police who were kind and explained in lay terms that she had a paranoid illness, later confirmed by my supervisor, who knew her well. What stays with me is how convincing detailed delusional systems can be, although I am aware that the possibility of real persecution exists.

Then came the long-awaited Child Care Course, then in its fourth year, run by Clare Britton (to become Winnicott). We were a small group of nine or ten, very diverse socially and academically.

Clare Britton was the dominant figure in the course in every respect. She was imbued with a huge enthusiasm for the task of educating a new kind of Child Care Officer and brought to it the experience of working with evacuated children during the War and other highly relevant work, including with groups for returning prisoners of war. I still remember her telling us of the mounting anxiety in those groups as mealtimes drew near, for men who had been starved. It is sadly impossible to recapture on paper the dynamics of Clare's teaching. For me, it was a kind of osmosis; perhaps the best kind. She was, quite simply, a brilliant teacher who presented issues and ideas freshly and with careful thought. The essentials for this professional career were laid for me at that stage. I was eager and open to learning of this kind.

Behind Clare lay the influence, notably, of her partner and husband-to-be, Donald Winnicott, who lectured to us. His style was more light-hearted than Clare's but there was the same spontaneity in presentation. He was witty, and quite enjoyed clowning, but always with a serious point in mind. He was an experienced paediatrician as well as a psychoanalyst, and his skill and sensitivity in the observation of mothers and infants in the Paddington Green clinic has had a permanent effect on the way I see these interactions.

I recall Donald Winnicott's simple drawing of a circle (womb) with a dot (baby) on the blackboard. As he spoke, he rubbed out bits of the chalk circle to show how the world impinges on the infant after birth; not being suddenly exposed to the full glare but gradually absorbing the stimuli now available to him or her. This is linked to the 'primary maternal preoccupation' of which he wrote; that is, the powerful protective, sheltering emotions of early motherhood. I was reminded later of this by the account of one of my students who had worked in Latin America, where the mother and new-born baby were kept in a dark hut for the first days of life.

These two people, Clare and Donald Winnicott, were the centre of my world at the LSE. They introduced us to the films of James and Joyce Robertson (1952), whose work in demonstrating the effects of maternal deprivation on young children were so influential. (I wonder how many of today's social workers realise that the now routine practice of 'going to hospital with mother' was a product of that work.)

All this was more than an educational experience, important as that was. It was an initiation into a way of looking at human interaction and of working out a professional role in the repair of damaged children which has left an indelible mark on me. Clare and Donald reinforced this by holding splendid parties in their tall, thin house in Victoria for present and past students. We were people whose clear task was to raise standards of child welfare in the country. There was lightness and fun at these parties, perhaps of particular value in those rather bleak post-war years.

There is more to say on my feelings about Clare and my relationship with her, which was at times prickly.

At this time, I was also introduced to a range of placements in field and residential work. As for nearly all social work students, these were very important to me, part of a process, I suppose, of confirming my professional identity and hence anxiety-provoking. These placements were thoroughly discussed with Clare, for whom we kept a diary. At that time, there were very few qualified Child Care Officers, so there was every likelihood that a student would have an unqualified supervisor; Clare's contribution was critical, therefore.

Two of the anxiety-provoking episodes stay with me. One was when the Children's Officer of Essex, Miss Wansborough-Jones, a formidable ex-civil servant, summoned me to her presence to deploy me to take charge of a children's home, where the officer in charge had left abruptly and the deputy had had a breakdown. I still recall lying in bed the first night, listening to the children breathing and wondering what I would do if something happened. The story gives an idea of the newness of all this, of the beginnings of a service which had perforce to work with scarce resources (like me).

More painful, though, was the beginning of my field work placement in Surrey with an unqualified worker. After a week or so, she told me that she thought I would not make a good social worker. I fled back to London to cry over Clare who was extremely professional (I wanted more comfort) and cleverly placed me instead with a most unusual qualified worker, who also had a PhD. Her name was Ursula Behr, a German Jewish refugee. She was comfortable with my urgent and powerful interest in the role and I was comfortable working with her. She was not threatened by my challenging (or rather cheeky) behaviour, which included, I seem to recall, teasing her that she took her hands off the steering wheel when she was talking. (She did.)

As with so much in my life, the fact that Ursula was Jewish was a strand in my long-term interest in Jewish people and their history. Not that Ursula talked of it but I had by then seen films of Auschwitz and was well aware of the Holocaust. When I met her mother, I made these connections. I greatly respected Ursula Behr. Best of all, she accepted me and engaged me as I was; that freed me to be myself.

A final reflection about my experience at the LSE concerns my choice of dissertation topic. Donald Winnicott's teaching had included references to 'transitional objects', the 'bits of stuff' to which babies and infants can become passionately attached and from which they are deeply distressed if separated. (These he styled as 'the first not-me objects'.) The choice of this as the subject of my dissertation was not linked, so far as I am aware, to specific experiences in my own childhood but the issue engaged my interest and enthusiasm. I constructed a modest research project; writing to *The Nursery World*, a weekly journal edited by Susan Isaacs who was also a psychoanalyst, I acquired fascinating letters from mothers describing their experiences with their infants and these objects which were often very strange and smelly. I also held groups in the East End and captured some of these experiences with working-class children. The result was a student dissertation which, to my utter amazement, ended in publication in the journal *Psycho-Analytic Study of the Child* (Stevenson, 1954). The crowning glory was an invitation to give it as a paper to the London meeting of psychoanalysts, chaired by Anna Freud. I arrived at her house, clad in my very best grey suit with pink blouse, with Clare; we walked up the steps and Anna Freud remarked in the familiar accent of the 'Hampstead refugees' of the time, 'And is zis very frightened young lady our guest?' I have little memory of the rest, except of a sea of faces of middle-aged, grey-haired women, who looked benign as I grew hotter and hotter.

I think it is probably fair to say that the initiative I showed in the work for the dissertation was unusual and, for someone at that stage in her career, it was a considerable achievement. However, it was not long before I found it an embarrassment; pomposity and purple prose were never far away and, most important, it is theoretically very weak, using but not successfully developing, Winnicott's own theory. I remember, years later, saying some of this to Clare; she remarked, 'I expect because it wasn't really your own', which was a perceptive and accurate comment. Still, I left that course with a distinction (though still, quite unreasonably, cross that I had only achieved a pass in the social studies diploma).

I cannot describe my time at the LSE as happy. My personal life was troubled and I was caught up in a very intense (and subsequently mutually destructive) relationship with another woman student social worker. I did not tell Clare Winnicott any of this; the secrecy and stigma surrounding lesbian relationships is something a younger generation can only now glimpse. But I did seek help from the student counsellor at the LSE. It was initially a relief for my sexuality to be accepted, especially after earlier totally unsatisfactory attempts to seek help. Looking back, I think my (male) counsellor was probably a skilled and kind therapist and it is unfortunate that one episode stands out vividly and hurtfully in my mind. I was on a rant about there being 'nothing wrong with being a lesbian' (or homosexual, as we then said). He agreed but added, 'It is, of course, sterile'. More than half a century later, that word is like a dagger. But I can see that my professional life has in fact mobilised sublimination very successfully. These were the days when lesbian women and babies did not go together and the very idea was unthinkable. I was perhaps fortunate in that I did not believe I had any choice and have not experienced the intense 'broody' feelings that so many women describe. But powerful maternal feelings were channelled into my work, particularly in relation to students in the next stage of my career. In any case, the concept of sterility is much wider than the procreation of children. Creativity can take many forms.

The Child Care Course laid the foundations for the rest of my career. Unfortunately, however, it was not rooted in good enough learning about the social and political context in which the developing profession of social work was located. In particular, hugely important issues of culture and class completely passed me by; I became very aware of such intellectual deficits when I first went to Oxford (Barnett House) to teach, in 1962. This was in the heyday of Chelly Halsey's sociological leadership at Barnett House. (I am not sure how much of such knowledge was in fact available at the LSE in 1953. Certainly, it played no part on the course.) I shall return to this issue later but first, there are the years 1954 to 1962, again crucial in consolidating a sense of professional identity.

5

Life as a Social Worker

Child Care Officer, Devon

From 1954 to 1958, I worked in Devon as a Child Care Officer. This was a deliberate choice, influenced, I suspect, by the links which Clare had fostered with Children's Officers and authorities she knew to be progressive. Kenneth Brill had by then moved to Devon from Croydon and doubtless remembered the intense young woman who had worked in one of his children's homes in Croydon. He offered me a post – very unusual at the time – in which a small proportion of my time was to be spent on 'research', undefined, for him.

For most of my time, I worked my Tiverton/Crediton area from Exeter doing all the usual work of a Child Care Officer. This included a high proportion of short-stay receptions into care of very young children, often when a mother was going into hospital. (There is much less of such work today, reflecting various social trends and changing professional practice.) I recall this work as having been very satisfying, when it went according to plan. To plan a foster home placement, to introduce a parent and children to a foster home, to take the children when the time came, to visit, to report back to parents and to take home again formed a coherent 'package of care' which, done well, engaged the skills of a new Child Care Officer. The teaching from the course was directly relevant, especially in relation to the needs of very young children. ('Not-me' possessions were never forgotten.) The bread and butter of the work – short-term admissions to care – brought me into contact with a wide variety of foster parents. Most of them lived in council houses; the men working in agriculture saw fostering as 'women's work' and we did not expect anything else from them. I had a sense of partnership with these women but found it hard to manage the rivalry between them and their keen observation of my car at any given house. Of course, this was assumed to be due to my preference for some rather than others. But my respect for the flexibility and good humour of those who took a series of children of all sorts was profound.

One woman in particular, Mrs E, had about thirty children during my time. She had boys of her own and managed these placements without apparent emotional difficulty. After I left, I heard with fascination, that she had 'fallen in love' with a baby girl placed from the local hospital for what were then termed 'mentally handicapped' girls and subsequently adopted her. This brought home to me that the dynamics of interaction between foster parents and different children may vary enormously.

It was extremely important that I could learn my trade in an organisation and under supervision which valued what I wanted to bring to the work. Behind Kenneth Brill lay the redoubtable figure of Nora Gallup, the Deputy Children's Officer, who worked in the Exeter office where I was located. All receptions into care had to be discussed thoroughly with her and I can still hear the loud bang of her name stamp as she read social workers' records in another part of the room. Nora Gallup had no professional training, which was usual at the time. She was a single, handsome woman, a product of an upper-class family and Roedean, with a booming voice and an absolute commitment to the children's well-being. She knew a lot about hardship, I think, although she said little about her feelings or family. She did once tell me that she had always had to wear boys' clothes, cast-offs from her elder brothers, and had never had enough to eat. I suspect nannies and absentee parents but she never said this. Thus, discussions of children coming into care with Nora followed a familiar pattern. One element concerned clothes and luggage. Never was I required to find clothes for these children in the (now defunct) 'county stores' in which rows and rows of identical little suits and frocks were to be used for deprived children. I went to the foster home waving vouchers for local shops. Nor was I ever required to reclaim the clothes after a placement. I thought this was really lovely and was a little surprised when these very poor parents were unenthusiastic about new clothes which they had not chosen coming back to them with the children. Furthermore, Nora insisted that children always travelled with their belongings in a suitcase. It grieves me that, in very recent years, I have heard of children moving into and out of care with black bin bags of possessions.

Another memory, of crucial importance, is that when talking about the pros and cons of more complex admissions to care, Nora always asked me, 'And what will happen to this child when he or she is eighteen?'

Nora drove an open-top, rather glamorous car, in striking contrast to our county-owned little unheated Fords, in which we drove hundreds of miles. I recall that in my first month of October she introduced me to the various Area Offices in other parts of Devon. One vivid and beautiful memory is of going to Tavistock with Nora and having my very first glimpse of autumnal Exmoor in all its purple glory. This is probably a somewhat idealised picture of Nora Gallup. But it is difficult to overestimate the importance of her crucial role in this first stage of my career development; nothing she said or did clashed with what I had taken from my training. Her firm and practical views gave form and substance to ideals. There was also a sense of being allowed to try new things. Quite soon I acquired two 'problem families' (a term much used at the time to describe families struggling with multiple difficulties) with whom I worked *very* intensively. In the 1950s, there was not an explicit legal framework for preventative work, although the Children Act 1948 stressed that children should not be taken into care unless all other avenues had been explored. It would have been easy for my interest in this aspect of the work to be discouraged, instead, it was facilitated. This feels extremely different from the experiences about which I hear today.

An important part of my work was with the parents of children in care. Two cases took up a great deal of my time; in one case, looking back, I think I was given too loose a rein and became over-involved. 'Mr H' was himself a child from the orphanage. His daughter had been committed to care because of his sexual abuse of her. I was tasked with sitting between him and his daughter if we went to the cinema and generally watching out when they were together. He was like a child himself and became very dependent on me. This resulted in the absurd situation of my meeting him at a stated place on Friday evenings for him to hand to me the payment owed to the local authority for his daughter's care. He said that that was the only way he could be sure the money would be spent on her. (I was anxious to avoid his descent into further trouble for non-payment.) I was fortunate that these curious exchanges were not misunderstood.

The second case, on reflection, gives me some lasting satisfaction. 'E' was a woman in her thirties, assessed as 'mentally handicapped'. 'E', in today's terms, might have been described as 'mildly learning disabled'; she could read and write and her records referred to family and social problems in her background. She had three children in care and another on the way. She was trapped in the deplorable policy of the times, whereby girls and young women were hospitalised, let out 'on licence' and recalled if they misbehaved. High on the list of misbehaviours was becoming pregnant. It seems more than likely that she was 'put away' for reasons connected with her background.

When I met her, she said to me, 'If you take this one away, I will only have another'. Given her track record, this seemed very likely. Her situation made a big impact on me. I could not challenge the policy, it was simply not within my power, although I do recall raising my doubts with the psychiatrist at the hospital. But I did find a foster home which would welcome her visits and help her to engage with her baby. Devon is a very big county and there were long car journeys to take her to see her lovely baby. Unfortunately 'E' was often car sick and we never managed to stop in time. I do recall on one occasion when a friend and colleague, Grace Yelland, generously offered to clean the car for me on my return.

It is the outcome of this case which still warms my heart. 'E' was still visiting when I left and she gave me a pair of pillowcases with a card thanking me for '… what you done and for all the other children you kindly look after'. To me, that spoke volumes, especially about her capacity to understand my role. I later learned that she agreed to the adoption of that baby boy by the foster mother, did not have more children, but made a home for two of her older sons and eventually married successfully. There are vital lessons to be learned from such a case. Some years later, I read with interest and admiration, Janet Mattinson's *Marriage and Mental Handicap* (1970) which described a number of such successful unions. I often think of 'E' and her many peers. We have moved away from such barbarous controls over people's lives. But it is ironic that I now find myself saddened and angered at the lack of support such women have when they are free to bring up their children. A high proportion of neglected children have mothers in that position and they may well be at serious risk in all kinds of ways.

There was a small research role which Kenneth Brill had set aside for me. I suspect that he had little idea of how to use me and that it was part of his plan to attract young, ambitious staff to the department. I was not experienced enough to realise how this would be viewed by others. My caseload was lower than that of others, always a fertile source of tension. I was not reticent about the role and gradually realised that I was resented by some. Again (as in the case of my first supervisor on the course) I was slow to recognise envy as a destructive force and lacking in awareness of the impact which I had on people.

However, there was one valuable outcome for me though I doubt whether it profited the department. For some years, I attended the case conferences every month on children in the Reception Home at Torquay. I took the minutes. It was a wonderful opportunity to see the progress (or lack of it) in the children who came into care. Some of this I reported in two short articles in the *Hospital and Social Services Journal*. Much more important was the grounding it gave me in persistent, careful observation of children in these circumstances. Another building block in my professional development.

Another facet of my Devon experience was a meeting, within the first few weeks, with a very tall, fit-looking young woman, who had arrived at the same time as I, as a Probation Officer in Exeter. With typical thoughtfulness, Nora Gallup introduced me to Phyllida Parsloe, fresh from Home Office training – as it then was – and a history graduate from Bristol University. (Two 'new girls' together.) Our friendship was immediate and, within a few months, we had found a flat together; subsequently we moved to a lovely little thatched cottage in Ebford, near Topsham, where we spent the next four years. (The rent being 4 Guineas a week, I recall.) That friendship has been very important to me throughout my life.

In relation to social work, there are particularly interesting elements. As we sped about the county in our similar, uncomfortable, Ford cars and brought home our daily doings, I learned for the first time some important lessons about the effect of professional role on perceptions of the work. Particularly memorable is a case which Phyllida held about which I had detailed knowledge. The 'C' family occupied a good deal of her time. Both parents had mild learning difficulties and had a succession of children whose names all began with P. Probation staff were involved when one of the babies was 'overlaid' in bed and died. The parents were placed on probation. Then a toddler got frost-bite when his foot was hanging out of the pram and the foot had to be amputated. Tensions rose as court proceedings were initiated. I knew that my boss wanted a care order; Phyllida (supported by *her* boss) wanted a supervision order. I saw for the first time the tension between different perspectives; between a view of parental needs and rights and a view of the child's well-being as paramount. Of course, it is all much more complicated than that; there was no 'Framework for Assessment', nor had we recognised that children were not always well served in care. But the important memory is that the parties were sincere and that there were real issues underlying organisational and professional dynamics.

A supervision order to the Probation Officer (then legally possible) was granted and my subsequent memories are of Phyllida taking on the task of supervising 'Mr and Mrs C' and the five little Cs, with her customary energy and commitment. No worry about giving Mrs C our home phone number, which she rang whenever the going got rough.

A vivid memory which both Phyllida and I share is of the evening when we had Clare and Donald Winnicott to dinner. This was An Event for us; best clothes and carefully chosen meal. In the middle, Mrs C rang, to Phyllida's intense embarrassment. She was shy and lacking in confidence at that time and to talk to Mrs C in the same room as our guests was, I guess, agony. Mrs C usually prefaced her remarks with, 'Oh, Miss Parsloe, I don't know what the end will be'.

In this cottage, too, we entertained June, a woman then in her twenties with Downs Syndrome. Her single, middle-aged mother was on probation for theft of blankets; a former nurse, she lived in a caravan, on benefits and had stolen out of desperation to care for her baby. June used to come to lunch occasionally, to give her totally isolated mother a break. It was the first time that I had been so close to anyone with a learning disability. I was uncomfortably aware of my distaste at her eating habits and have thought about that over and over again when I have had similar encounters. I also learned, through Phyllida, the support that it is possible (and necessary) to give women in such a position. Such work is no longer part of a Probation Officer's role. I would like to believe that the development of adult services ensures that the needs of June and her mother would now be met in a different way. I fear I cannot be sure of this.

A further important work connection with Phyllida was focussed on a Devon County Council school for 'maladjusted' children run by Guy and Peggy Willatts. Such schools (of about thirty children) were a fairly common provision for emotionally and socially disturbed children. My own interests in such provision had, of course, been initiated by my work at The Mulberry Bush in Oxfordshire. Guy and Peggy were entirely different from the Dockar-Drysdales and had little theoretical backing or training in the work. They were supremely gifted in the care of difficult and unhappy children, mostly teenagers. Guy was a mild mannered man, who had spent considerable time as an army officer during the

War; he met Peggy, also in the army, and they enjoyed a fund of stories about all of that. I think Peggy carried most of the anxiety for them both in their caring for 'risky children'. Guy had one outstanding quality: he was totally unthreatened by the behaviour of these young people, including their sexual overtures or exhibitionism towards him. No doubt, by today's risk-averse standards, he may have been insufficiently concerned to protect himself. But it worked. Guy and Peggy, who had no children and had married late, established lasting and in some cases life-long relationships with these 'maladjusted' children. Indeed, I heard that just before Peggy died (she had dementia in her last years), a group of the women who had been her 'maladjusted' clientele came together to help her.

Phyllida and I both had responsibility for children at this school. There were a number who were the subject of care orders and so the Children's Department took responsibility for their overall welfare, including holiday provision. It was here that I first encountered a broken adoption; the boy, adopted by a Royal Air Force officer and his wife, sadly became the victim of middle-class family dysfunction. It was a vivid, early example to me that family difficulties cross class boundaries.

Phyllida and I became friends of the Willatts and mixed pleasure with work in an entirely unselfconscious way, discussing the children at length before going on to lighter matters and a gin and tonic (their favourite tipple). I learned so much from this, not least a powerful respect for people who can do so well the kind of work which involves intense, daily contact with difficult and unhappy children.

Writing about my friendship with Phyllida reminds me that, throughout my working life, my professional life had been enriched by close friendships and intimate relationships. My commitments to work were so powerful and time consuming that it is hardly surprising that most of my most important relationships began from working contacts. There are negative and positive aspects of that.

One further strand to the rich Devon experience was being asked to supervise a student who had failed in her previous placement. I flung myself into this with great interest and enthusiasm, with a successful outcome. Looking back, it is clear to me that the foundations of a career change were laid there. I had long resented my father's attempts to encourage me towards teaching. Yet I had a talent for it and this first supervisory experience brought together social work and teaching in a way which I found very satisfying.

After four years in Devon, I became restless, and guilty about being restless. I felt that I needed to move but it seemed arrogant even to wonder whether I had learned as much as I could. I shared these anxieties with a Home Office inspector who came to review my work. I recall a feeling of intense relief and gratitude when he said it was only to be expected!

In 1958, it was time to move on, taking with me experience, supervision and support from a good department which has stood me in good stead for the rest of my professional life.

6

Further Professional Development

The Tavistock Clinic, London 1958/1959

At this time, too, Phyllida left Devon; I went to do the Advanced Social Casework course at the Tavistock Clinic, she to the LSE to qualify as a psychiatric social worker. Looking back, my move to the Tavistock Clinic in 1958 seems predictable. I wanted fresh professional stimulus and the psychoanalytic basis of the work at the clinic built on my earlier learning with the Winnicotts.

We were a small group of social work students including two Probation Officers, diverse in background and experience. Each student carried a small case-load and worked along the familiar lines of fifty-minute clinic interviews with parent(s) once a week, very fully recorded (in every detail), followed by supervision. This was the core of the course. I was extremely disappointed not to have as my supervisor Elizabeth Irvine, a distinguished social work scholar. My supervisor did not fulfil my hopes and expectations; impossible to tell whether this was coloured by my (ambitious) resentment at not being given 'the best' as I saw it. But, certainly, there was not a meeting of minds. Nonetheless, the experience gained was a very useful contrast to the free and easy home visiting in Devon. I learned something about discipline; even more important, I began to see that these focussed interviews could provide a structure in which the underlying theme or need which the client brought could be explored. Also, tentatively, I began to understand something of the process of transference and counter-transference which is present even in the less intense encounters in social work.

In all this, I was helped by a friendship with Isca Wittenberg-Salzberger, who was training as a psychoanalyst. She was much influenced by Melanie Klein, subsequently publishing a book for social workers on that theory (Wittenberg-Salzberger, 1970). My discussions with her went a long way to make up for the disappointment over supervision.

Although I have not adopted Kleinian theory in any wholesale way, the course at the Tavistock Clinic allowed me to consolidate my long-standing interest in direct work with children; an important part of Melanie Klein's own work. Part of our course was child observation of a group of toddlers at the Tavistock Nursery. These were children of parents who were keen for their children to have experiences based on Tavistock principles. (If there was also observation of infants, I have forgotten.) We then discussed our observations with Frances Tustin, a psychoanalyst whose specialism was the study of autism, then little talked about. I found those discussions exciting and illuminating and recollections of them are to be found in my first book *Someone Else's Child* (1964).

The ten-month course at the Tavistock Clinic was an intense experience. Being on the fringe of a group of people so totally absorbed in the psychoanalytic world was always going to be emotionally disturbing. And my personal life was in some turmoil. I did not at this time seek more therapy myself – that was later – but I did a good deal of vicarious learning. Most importantly, the ethos of the Tavistock did not breed arrogance or self-approval. Rather it helped to place us firmly in the human family with all the powerful emotions to beset us as much as our clients. For me, Kleinian theory offered me a new understanding of the distinction between envy and jealousy and the destructive power of the former because 'I want what you've got'. I was helped by this to manage others' envy of me but also to learn how destructive I could be when this emotion came into play.

In such a centre as the Tavistock the most powerful emotions were leaking out all over the place, especially amongst those in analysis. The vigorous voices of mittel-European Jewish analysts were the norm and fascinated me; I was privileged to visit Isca Wittenberg-Salzberger's family when her sister died and to join them in mourning.

I liked the lively, even aggressive discussions I overheard at the Tavistock. Coming from my inhibited suburban background, there was something strange and exotic about all this. Perhaps it is not surprising that, in my mind, I set these experiences against seminars with John Bowlby, whose manner, voice and clothes were indistinguishable from those of a colonial administrator. Indeed I recall an end-of-term party (how the staff must have hated it) when the student playing John Bowlby wore a colonial topee throughout. I have often thought of him since; his combination of biological sciences and psychoanalytic theory makes his contribution unique. The ideas which he developed, now known as 'attachment theory' (Bowlby, 1997), were to be fundamental in the development of social work practice. He had a kind of 'groundedness' which kept his theory rooted in earthly reality when other theoretical balloons lost their moorings. For example, pictures of lines of ducklings following a quasi-mother cardboard box helped.

7

A Social Work Academic: Early Years

Lecturer in Social Work, Bristol University (1959/1961)

So it was time for the next phase. A curious and serendipitous connection was to prove very important. Throughout my undergraduate years, I made one close and lasting friend, Karina, whom I first met at interview. As I got to know her better, I learned that she had been nurtured as a child (with a difficult family background) by a group of women; one was Sybil Clement-Brown, a psychiatric social worker, who worked in the Home Office when the Child Care Courses began and who interviewed me in 1953 and approved me for grants to the LSE. Another was Susan Isaacs, a psychoanalyst, who for a while edited *The Nursery World*, one of the sources of my data for my LSE dissertation on 'transitional objects'. Susan was married to Karina's uncle and was also much involved in her upbringing. By a strange coincidence, I found myself being interviewed by Karina's uncle, Nathan Isaccs, for funding a small research project when my time at the Tavistock Clinic was ending. This was made possible on professional psychoanalytic grapevine and had nothing to do with Karina.

Karina's uncle was an able scientist. After all these years, I still recall being daunted by his approach to research, rooted in the empirical tradition of which I had no knowledge. It was a kind of glimmering understanding that description was not the same as evidence and it made me uncomfortable. So, an energetic, but extremely naïve young woman presented her so-called research plan to Nathan Isaacs. He chaired the Susan Isaacs Research Fellowships Trust. I perceived in his questioning 'Big Issues' which I did not really comprehend. With some hesitation, I believe, he nonetheless gave me a half salary for a year to pursue my ideas. In 1959, I went to Bristol University with Lulie Shaw as my boss, on a half-time basis; first as tutor to the new Child Care Course, with my research project as the other half.

The research would not now stand up to scrutiny. It consisted of interviews with foster mothers of very young children and its (somewhat vague) objectives were to understand better the feelings and reactions of children and adults. Like many before and since, I did not find it easy to focus on this research, combining working on a new course with a new role. For some years, the unfinished research hung uneasily over my conscience. However, the eventual outcome, which utilised that work (and other experience) was my first book, *Someone Else's Child*, first published in 1964. The title was a good one. I knew by then that I needed to address the tensions between the adults who cared for children and the book was an attempt to see things from three different perspectives: children, foster parents and parents. The book also sought to explain some of the current policies and trends in child care. I had decided that the book was to be directed primarily at foster parents and I used a direct first-person style, a speaking style, to facilitate this. I was enraged when, on receiving the proofs, I found the style had been altered throughout from 'you' to 'they'. I fought and won that battle!

In the event, the book was read as much by social workers as foster parents; this was probably because of the large numbers of non-graduates who entered social work in this period. Many of them had not studied much before and the book seemed to speak to their needs. It was reprinted in 1977 and had steady sales over many years. It has, of course, dated but I am not now ashamed of it or embarrassed by it. There was a period when, new to Oxford as an academic, I felt awkward about it; also, I was conscious of the unsatisfactory research which had preceded it. But it shows well my intense interest in child development and behaviour and my involvement in contemporary child welfare. And I am good at explaining difficult matters clearly. Past important professional influences from the LSE, Devon, the Tavistock Clinic, and the Universities of Bristol and Oxford were to be found in this book by the time it emerged in 1964. Nor was my study of English literature without influence, an important element in the vicarious understandings of what it may mean to be a child. For example, questions such as: 'How does a little child see the grownups around him?... You [the adult] must seem so big; he/she has to lift his/her head to see your face.' The writer Laurie Lee describes in his book *Cider with Rosie* (1959) how he felt lost in the long grass which he saw 'towering' above him and 'all around' him and in 'Clouds of Glory' (1962), the poet Lawrence Durrell, writing from a baby's perspective, speaks of adults' fingers which seem like beanstalks, chins which are like balconies and kisses which are like 'black thunder'. So – you, the adult, are big and you are powerful.

Whilst this research moved slowly on, I embarked on the first years of what was to be a lifetime in social work education. Lulie Shaw, one of the many psychiatric social workers who contributed to the early days of social work as a profession, was by then a woman in her fifties. She was a Quaker, an elegant, good-looking woman, deeply reserved. The new social work course was situated in the Economics Department for the University; my colleague Barbara Butler, who had been an undergraduate at Lady Margaret Hall at the same time as me, was a figure of some mystery. (Did she foster that?) There were, I recall, nine women students in that first year and I flung myself into the tutorial role. Fresh from the Tavistock, I was rather too preoccupied with the unconscious and I fear my students suffered as a result. I was, however, pleased to go to a reunion of the group more than thirty years later and to find that, in their different ways, most of these women had contributed over many years to social work or related fields. It is difficult to convey how alien social work felt embedded in an economics department. Perhaps it is best conveyed by my meeting the Professor of Economics (rarely seen) as I was leaving the building on a rainy day. He looked at me kindly and said, 'Hello Miss Stevenson, rotten weather for your kind of work'. (In the field?)

Lecturer & Reader in Applied Social Studies, Barnett House, University of Oxford (1962–1976)

My time at Bristol coincided with a surge in training for social work, especially child care. My post was temporary and part-time, though I believe Lulie Shaw was seeking a way to appoint me to a full-time post. At that time, three new courses, of eighteen-month duration, for graduates from any subject were approved by the Home Office. These courses were at the universities of Nottingham, Birmingham and Oxford. In 1962, I was appointed to the University of Oxford, to Barnett House, the Department for Social and Administrative Studies as Lecturer in Applied Social Studies, a move which proved to be of huge importance to my professional and academic development.

Those years – until 1976 – were ones of intense activity; they were very productive. They were also a period of great difficulty personally. The death of my mother in 1966 precipitated me back into a relationship from which I had painfully extricated myself some years before. That led to near disaster; from that I went into other relationships, all fraught with tension and pain. Once again, as has been the pattern throughout my life, friendships and intimate relationships were inextricably bound up with work. At that time, it was far from easy to acknowledge myself as a lesbian and, although I never denied it, I did not formally 'come out'. A kind of social denial was then common; such relationships amongst middle-class women were often tacitly acknowledged by those close to the people concerned. But nothing was ever said. In relation to the world of social work, I realise now that I endured a kind of uneasiness about how others saw me or what was said about me. I recall a moment when a student told me that her supervisor thought I was a lesbian.

(Shock horror!) I was indignant at the gossip rather than the charge. I was fortunate that I never became involved with a student.

Barnett House had a long and honourable tradition of bringing great awareness of social deprivation to the more privileged classes in society. Its origins lay in the nineteenth-century settlement movement, in which clergy and academics from various parts of Oxbridge founded establishments, mainly in the poorest parts of London. Canon Barnett had been one of those. At the time of my arrival at Barnett House, there were already two courses, one for personnel managers and one for basic social sciences. The eighteen-month course was to combine basic social science with social work training for graduates with 'non-relevant' degrees. The ludicrous eighteen-month length was no doubt the consequence of a compromise over funding at the Home Office. It was ludicrous because it took no account of the student overlap in the staff-student ratios and placed impossible demands on us. (These courses did not last long.)

I was happy and excited to return to Oxford, where I had enjoyed very good undergraduate days. Planning and designing the course was exhilarating. At this time, Oxford City Council and Oxfordshire County Council had separate children's departments, with Lucy Faithfull and Barbara Kahan as their distinguished Children's Officers. They were considered prestigious departments to work in and I was fortunate in being able to recruit some excellent practice teachers. Lucy Faithfull welcomed me warmly and my relations with her were cordial throughout her life; it was less easy with Barbara Kahan.

At the end of my first year at Barnett House, a new Head was appointed whose impact on my life and development was considerable. This was Professor Alexander 'Chelly' Halsey, who came from Birmingham; he was a distinguished sociologist whose work on social class and education was well known. The early years of his tenure were marked by an explosion of research, funded by a Labour government, in which he played a leading part. So we had the Educational Priority Areas and the Community Development Projects research. This ran alongside my own, less prestigious activities and I had no direct contact with it, although I was very interested. (Later, I came to think that I was not wanted.) But it was an exciting time and it exposed me for the first time to debate about research methods in the social sciences, to able social scientists, and, better late than never, to sociology as a discipline. I recall asking Chelly Halsey if he would give me some sociology tutorials. He said no. I have never understood why. So I had a private academic struggle in order to try to bring together, not to integrate, the knowledge base from psychoanalytic theory with that of sociology for the purpose of social work. One outcome of this was the rather pompous article on 'Knowledge for Social Work' published in the *British Journal of Social Work* (1971). It became absolutely clear to me that we needed a range of theoretical insights for social work to develop. But this has always been and continues to be, an extremely difficult idea to put into action. (I recall, later, a colleague who presented a theory a week for ten weeks to the students with predictably confused results.)

So what can I now pick out about the Oxford course (which was lengthened to two years during this period)? There were, I think, four characteristics which marked it out; this is confirmed by various discussions and reunions with past students over the years. One was the calibre of students; those motivated to apply to Oxford were, by and large, able and brought with them good degrees. They were also highly motivated socially, caught up in the Welfare State's ideals, but not very (party) politically active. There were lively, innovative young people and I loved working with them.

Those same students have told me over the years how much they valued the quality of the academic teaching which they received. Nowhere else that I subsequently worked could draw on the services of so many able academics. High on their list for praise was Nigel Walker, then Professor of Criminology at Nuffield. There are a number of such names. Thus this was, by and large, a period when the needs and strengths of the students were well met by the academics.

The students also remembered, with many tales and much laughter, 'the play groups' as being of great importance in their development. These were my idea, borne out of earlier experiences, including those at the Tavistock Clinic. We had groups on two Oxford housing estates, Barton and Blackbird Leys. These were run by the students in groups, once a week, for school-aged children and were followed by discussion (supervision) with tutors. There were the usual problems of selecting the children (how deprived did they have to be to qualify?) and of discipline. Looking back, it all seems like another era. Without a care for 'Health and Safety' of children, students or buildings, without any discussion of child protection or safeguarding, the students sallied forth and played with the children. There were moments of anxiety, as when small boys peed from the roof, and so on. But, years later, the message has come back to me that for many students this was the first time that they had met and interacted with children in this way and its effects were long lasting. History does not tell us what the children felt but I can't think it did them any harm.

In subsequent years, in the rushed expansion of social work courses, both quantitatively and in curriculum content, these opportunities were lost. This is now seen as a matter of regret and there have been some attempts to re-introduce comparable elements for student learning through direct observation and interaction. But there are setbacks. It is arguable that much of the poor quality of direct work with children which has been noted in recent research and literature, including Serious Case Reviews, can be traced back to the demise of this type of practice experience.

Finally, in identifying the characteristics which gave the Barnett House course a good name in the early days, the development of practice placements and supervisory skills were well to the fore. It was not dominated by the academic ethos; allowing for rose-tinted spectacles, it seems to me to have found a good balance between the academic and the professional and between the use of the intellect and the use of feelings. I was very interested in the processes of learning and teaching and supervisors' meetings which explored the techniques of 'process recording', a skill that is now little valued in social work practice. (I still have some of the papers about this.) It was at this time that I first encountered the work of a (then) well-known educationalist A.N. Whitehead, and was caught up in the idea of applying his work on the stages of learning to social work. Briefly, he proposed three stages: romance, generalisation and precision. The journey of learning music by ear, through learning to read music and applying it to the concentration on the detail, to the particularity of the composition being played, seems to me to bear comparison to the process of professional social work education.

However, there was turbulence in my private life and this played a part in my rather unlikely decision in 1968 to apply for a temporary post as Social Work Advisor to the Supplementary Benefits Commission (SBC), based in London.

Social Work Advisor, the Supplementary Benefits Commission, London (1968)

Even at this distance, I cannot really be sure of the extent to which my decision to join the Supplementary Benefits Commission (SBC) as Social Work Advisor was personal or career-driven. I had absolutely no knowledge of the workings of the wider social security system, nor of the SBC. The SBC was a quango, independent of government but inextricably bound up with it. It had replaced the National Assistance Board, set up in 1947. Very broadly, its powers were concerned with means-tested benefits, rather than those to which citizens were entitled 'by category', for example, the basic state pension. It had inherited all the tensions surrounding the means test; pre-war memories of the humiliation of poor people who had to claim such benefits hung heavily on the shoulders of the Commissioners. I believe that there was sincere concern to dispel these memories and it seems probable that the appointment for the first time of a Social Work Adviser was part of that concern. (It would be interesting to see the government papers which were circulated concerning this.) There was something about the challenge which appealed to me, despite my ignorance. Reflecting on my career, it is clear that there are two aspects of it which recur; one is that I was up for a challenge; the second, and more important, is that I was fascinated by the possibility of making links between different issues. This job offered such an opportunity. Nor was it opposed by Chelly Halsey, whose long association with politics and policy in London made him, as were so many academics living in Oxford, quite comfortable with such excursions. Looking back, I was not grateful enough for the way in which he eased my transition to a job which was originally for a year but extended to nearly two.

My task at the SBC was to prepare for the Commissioners a series of papers on the key elements of their work, for example, those concerning lone mothers, so-called 'voluntarily unemployed men', the work of special welfare officers whose case-load comprised people whose problems did not fit the system, and so on. (I recall a difficult issue as to whether a transsexual could have special payments for make-up.) In short, the topics were appropriately chosen in the correct assumption that there was likely to be a 'social work angle' on them.

I was an oddity in the system and the Civil Service did not know how to cope with me. The level of expenses, kind of room and secretarial assistance to which I was entitled epitomised this difficulty and had perhaps a wider significance – the amount of influence I could be expected to have. For example, I recall being told of anxious phone calls when regional managers rang HQ to inquire whether my visit necessitated a VIP lunch or sandwiches at the pub. My line manager was Tony Crocker, an under secretary, without whom I guess I would have blundered much more often. Tony was a veteran of the Arnhem parachute disaster, had lost a limb and heaved himself about on a very heavy prosthesis. He had a bad stutter which did not seem to worry him and smoked a pipe incessantly, his hands always grubby from the matches and relighting. He was in the very best sense of the word, a gentleman, with innate courtesy and sense of humour. Some time after I had left the SBC, I brought to him the draft of my book, *Claimant or Client? A Social Worker's View of the Supplementary Benefits Commission* (1972) which represented the fruits of my labours there. Looking back, I am deeply grateful for the skill with which he helped me convey my own messages without running up against the Official Secrets Act or other resistance to publication. I learned from him that there are ways of wording sensitive matters which avoid Big Trouble. I fear, however, it would be much more difficult in today's climate. Tony and I became friends and I visited him and his wife at home afterwards. Indeed, we exchanged Christmas cards for many years.

When I first went to the SBC, I sent for the papers of my only, long time ago, predecessor in such an advisory role, Eileen Younghusband, who was not herself a social worker (see Chapter 9). In 1947, she had been asked to examine the role of the (then) new National Assistance Board. The comments which jumped out of the page concerned the difference which the National Health Service had made to poor people. She showed graphically how before 1947, the costs of illness weighed on people's lives, especially those of the elderly. Overnight, it seemed, the creation of the NHS changed the main focus of benefit claims. I have never forgotten this and am reminded of it when I read of those in the United States who are trapped by uninsurable healthcare.

For me, this period was exhilarating. I was learning a huge amount, very fast. I travelled the length and breadth of the country, visiting offices and paying home visits to every kind of individual and family.

There were a few surreal moments, for example when a local office manager invited me to his home for supper with his wife and daughter. After a conventional meal (tomato soup and steak and kidney pudding, I think), the daughter, aged about ten or eleven said, 'Daddy, can we listen to our rugger songs with Miss Stevenson?' He replied, 'Yes dear, of course'. Mother went out to do the washing up and I listened to some very coarse, not to say obscene, songs in this polite, well-ordered milieu. It offered me my first serious entrée into the world of social policy.

Back in London, I began to understand the underlying political tensions in these services. I was caught up in the battles of resources and public attitudes towards claimants who many called 'undeserving'. Looking back, what were the most important lessons of those two years?

This was the first time I had worked within an organisation which had all the hallmarks of a classic bureaucracy. The SBC was modelled on the typical government department with clearly defined hierarchies, an overriding preoccupation with fairness, i.e., treating people within given categories alike, underpinned by a wish for clear policies which would aid implementation. Its front-line officials were not formally encouraged to use initiative; nor did most of them resent it if their decisions were 'appealed' and perhaps overturned by their seniors. This was in striking contrast to my experience of social workers.

As the months went by, I realised that this was a setting in which social workers (or their equivalent) would find it very hard to function. It took me on a hugely important intellectual journey, resulting in my book *Claimant or Client? A Social Worker's View of the Supplementary Benefits Commission* (1972). This book was essentially about different forms of social justice and how they operated in the worlds of social welfare and social work. These issues had been explored by distinguished scholars such as John Rawls but I chose to use the theologian Paul Johannes Tillich to describe the same phenomenon in different words. Tillich (1960) wrote of 'creative or proportional justice'; two kinds of fairness, the former attuned to the differing needs of individuals, the latter to ensure that people with the same needs get equitable treatment. It is obvious that both are needed in a humane society.

The SBC was a striking case example of the dilemmas which this imperative creates. It was not part of the wider social security system which paid pensions, family allowances and so on. Within that system, 'proportional justice' must be seen to rule. It was set up to administer means-tested benefits, the 'extra' benefits which could be claimed by the poor. As with the wider social security system, it had to have a strong element of proportional justice, so that, once entitlement was established, benefits were calculated on the basis of specific allowances per child and per person in the household. But the nearer one got to individuals, the more their circumstances and therefore their needs were seen to vary and to require elements of 'creative justice'. In this way, the systems tended to become more complex and more refined. Thus, people found to have a disability were to be treated differently from those who were 'voluntarily unemployed' (the jargon of the time). Those whose needs were particular to their circumstances had 'exceptional needs payments', such as for special diets. Those beset by a crisis (for example, fire or flood) might have lump-sum grants. There were innumerable examples of this kind. The harsh truth was that the more simple the system (rough justice), the less likely it was to meet satisfactorily the varied and complex situations of the claimants. Yet – and still to this day – there is often public outcry for simplification of the rules. The over-long form is the classic target.

What I learned then, I have seen over and over again, especially during the years 1980 to 2000 when I was a member of the Social Security Advisory Committee. The ultimate in initiating complexity was to be seen over more than twenty years in the administration of cold-weather payments to elderly and disabled people. Every year there were arguments and refinements in the interests of 'creative justice'. Thus, it was not enough to prevent people from freezing to death; 'wind-chill' had to be introduced as an additional justification. Payments had to be calculated regionally, for obvious reasons. But how? Weather stations formed part of the map. Grants could be paid only after a certain number of days when temperatures fell continuously. But for how long? Did the very old need more than the merely old? Only in very recent times have these payments been simplified so that means-testing does not form part of the assessment. But the complexities are still there. This is simply an example of the enduring dilemmas in striving for a strong and just society in which social inequality is entrenched. Cold-weather payments reflect wider problems of poverty in certain groups.

Nonetheless, tension between these two kinds of justice seems inherent in a civilised society. We are in danger if we slip too far one way or the other. An example of this, of direct relevance to social work, concerns the criminal justice system, whether adult or juvenile. Justice requires that those who commit the same or similar offences should be treated equally, hence the 'tariff'; but it also requires that the condition or situation of the individual offender is taken into account.

To those who are knowledgeable in social philosophy, my enthusiasm about these concepts must seem naïve. But, for me, these notions of creative and proportional justice shaped my thinking over the years, whether it is operating within a family, an organisation or a state. In aspects of social welfare which concern financial help, it raises thorny questions as to how this is to be organised. This is exemplified in the unsatisfactory provisions over the years for individuals or families who experience particular financial difficulties at certain times. The SBC struggled with this and it has never been satisfactorily resolved. We have had legislation since which permits local authorities to make grants in certain circumstances. But these systems were never adequately developed. Logic suggests that central government, in the form of social security and allied provisions, could be the right place for 'fairness' in proportional terms to be located; indeed that is where it rests in our system. Local government, who carry the responsibility for direct work with individuals and families in difficulty, would be best placed to attend also to their unique financial needs, practising 'creative fairness'. But that omits the political tensions and battles for power between central and local government. It is easy to see why local government, depending so much on central government for finance, would fear the implication of assuming significant responsibilities of this kind. Thus, for over nearly forty years, there has been a continuous, rumbling discontent with the arrangements in place for the exercise of creative financial justice. The present Social Fund, centrally controlled, is a shocking example of punitive compromise, whereby most claimants are offered loans for particular needs or items and are then required to repay them out of basic state benefits. It is morally indefensible.*

During the time I was at the SBC, I was aware that different countries had developed social security systems in different ways. In some, basic benefits were administered at local level (as had, of course, once been the case in the United Kingdom). In such countries, as social work emerged as an occupation, social workers

---

* From 1 April 2013 the Social Fund as part of a nationally administered benefits system has ended and the resources transferred to local authorities to administer as they decide is appropriate.

became responsible for the day-to-day administration of the benefits. The combination of both kinds of justice did not work well and the 'categorical' or proceduralised aspect of the work became dominant. (Some comparable difficulties can now be seen in community care, where a shortage of resources has led to bureaucratisation of decision-making.)

I was invited during my time with the SBC to go to Israel and Hong Kong, both of which were introducing new systems of social security. For Hong Kong, still a colony in those days, it was a major step, however rudimentary, to provide a form of public assistance. It was not underpinned by any form of pension, unemployment benefit or health service.

The invitations came from different sources; the Israeli government were responsible for the first, the then Minister had been to the UK and was impressed by the workings of the Supplementary Benefits Commission. The invitation from Hong Kong came from the Professor who was responsible for social work education in the University of Hong Kong. That visit laid the foundations for important links with Hong Kong which have spanned forty years and developed in many ways.

My book, *Claimant or Client?* (1972) was an attempt to distil my thinking over the period between 1968 and 1970. Re-reading it, I think it was a good effort and it certainly came from my head and heart being engaged fully in the enterprise. It came as a shock to me, therefore, to realise that there were critics who believed it to be too derivative, too dependent on the work and thinking of Richard Titmuss (whose seminal article on the exercise of discretion was fully acknowledged in the book). The critics came from the world of social policy. There were a cluster of expert and very able social policy academics in the fields of health and social security and some may have viewed my enthusiastic and naïve intrusion into their space as rather annoying. I was not then aware of the awkward boundary between social work and social policy academics, epitomised at the LSE where the twain rarely met. (Separate tables in the dining room were usual.) To some extent, this has dogged the rest of my career. (Neither fish, fowl, nor good red herring.) But the truth is that my academic position is located between two worlds and it is there that I feel most comfortable.

Readership & Professorial Scholarship, St Anne's College, Oxford (1970)

Meanwhile, whilst I was ending my secondment with the SBC, there was plotting going afoot on my behalf of which I had no knowledge whatever. (It is impossible to imagine this happening now.) The Director of Barnett House, Chelly Halsey, organised my promotion to a Readership in Applied Social Studies, supported, I later learned, by a reference from Eileen Younghusband. I had given no thought to promotion at this stage of my career and it was, I guess, the most exciting event in my academic life. As soon as the news was out, I was offered Fellowships at two women's colleges. Up to this time, those of us (mostly scientists and social scientists) who were appointed by University faculties, not colleges, had no automatic right to a college fellowship and many were excluded. My Readership opened the door and I was thrilled to accept a Professorial Fellowship at St Anne's College. That appointment played a significant part in my life, personally and academically. I had also become much more aware of the significance of large scale research for academic development, from watching the sociologists at Barnett House and Nuffield College as they grappled with the Educational Priority Areas and Community Development programmes initiated by the government. It was not therefore surprising that I utilised my own experience within the SBC to acquire a substantial research grant into the so-called 'voluntarily unemployed' which was to explore the characteristics and problems of such claimants, in an era of relatively high unemployment.

It is very hard, even at this late stage in my life, to really understand the difficulties which were to ensue over the next few years, in my relationship with Chelly Halsey which were never made explicit and which were an important factor in my leaving Oxford. Chelly had been entirely responsible for securing me the Readership, for which I have always been grateful and which gave me a solid foundation of confidence in my chosen career. Did I then behave *too* confidently, even cockily? Did I represent (to him) a challenge in his leadership or authority? This was not intentional on my part. Indeed, over the years, I have found myself wanting to revere, even idealise, men in authority of an age to have been my brother. (I know this to be bound up with my relationship with my brother, who was seven years older than I.) What eventually became apparent was that there were two research empires in Barnett House, which did not collaborate or even exchange ideas, which could have been so fruitful.

The period spent in London and for two years after that were also important for me personally. I went into analysis with a Jungian, Judith Hubback, who helped to hold me steady through a crisis in a relationship which had revived after the death of my mother. On reflection, the therapeutic relationship which I experienced was peculiarly valuable for me because her excellent intellect was used in the service of feelings and not against them, as can happen in academic life. In this sense, Judith Hubback confirmed the earlier influences of Clare and Donald Winnicott on my development, on the way in which I saw social work and wanted to teach it. How best, in seeking to help others, to use one's mind and one's feelings together, has remained a central preoccupation of my professional life.

By 1972, then, I was an established senior academic, whose horizons had been hugely widened by the London secondment and subsequent research. I was finding my feet in the world of social policy as well as social work and I was exhilarated by my new place in St Anne's College as a Professorial Fellow, a (then) women's college. I relished that world of able, argumentative women, who included in their number a fair share of eccentrics, of whom splendid stories can be told. I particularly liked the tale of the Fellow who was persuaded to come to a Governing Body meeting, where her vote was needed, whilst she was on sabbatical leave. She came under protest with a pile of books and earplugs and pursued her studies until the relevant item on the agenda was reached.

However, difficulties were awaiting me which were to challenge me in profound ways, both personally and professionally.

8

The Maria Colwell Inquiry

In 1973, I was invited by the Department of Health and Social Security (DHSS) to become a member of the inquiry into the death of Maria Colwell. Maria was seven when she died at the hands of her stepfather William Kepple. The family lived in Brighton. This was to be the first of a stream of inquiries, now known as Serious Case Reviews, into the deaths or serious injuries to children to find out if the relevant agencies had provided the proper and necessary support. I had no idea at that stage of the significant part it would play in shaping subsequent policy nor had I any experience of such matters to guide me.

The Committee, set up by the then Secretary of State, Barbara Castle, was comprised of the Chair, Thomas Field-Fisher QC, Mrs Davey, an alderman of Essex County Council and me. There was little, if any, precedent to draw on in setting it up and the procedures were quite formal and legalistic. This has been mirrored in some of the better known subsequent inquiries, such as the Cleveland inquiry in 1988 (DHSS, 1988) and the Victoria Climbié inquiry in 2002 (DHSS, 2003), both of which were instituted by the government. However, most of the hundreds of similar inquiries since then have not adopted such procedures.

The Colwell inquiry was held in public; there was legal representation for the Committee as well as for the representatives of the various agencies who gave evidence. Although at the outset of the inquiry, not all the agencies giving evidence had legal representation. I think the Education Department was the first. Since the committee had its own barrister to put questions to witnesses, it was probable that agencies would follow suit, although Social Services did not.

The inquiry adopted formal court procedures and the court rose as we walked in. The case had aroused great interest in Brighton and nationally. We quickly realised that some of those who came day by day to hear the proceedings were, to put it mildly, somewhat strange and we were rather alarmed to find one of them prowling around for mementoes such as our name plates, to put in a (planned) museum about Maria Colwell.

We met in Brighton for nine weeks, hearing from a succession of agencies about the sad story of Maria. Looking back, it is almost impossible to recapture how strange this was for all of us, Committee included. The Chair, experienced in the criminal law, had not conducted such an inquiry before and had no expert knowledge in the matters of child welfare we were pursuing. Mrs Davey, though a former member of a Local Government Children's Committee in Essex, appeared to me to lack confidence and seemed rather overawed by the whole business. I knew a good deal about child welfare but had very little experience of legal matters or 'court' processes.

The stage was set for a clash between me and the Chair (Thomas Field-Fisher QC), who I am sure regarded me as opinionated and over-assertive. One of the factors which contributed to this friction was that he regarded us – and used us – as advisors to a judge rather than acknowledging that we had equal contributions to make. (That included an intention to write the report by himself.) There was a fundamental difference between us in how we saw and interpreted the same evidence. Our values were fundamentally incompatible, especially in relation to the apportionment of blame (both to parents and to agencies). Furthermore, he showed little or no awareness of the social and cultural milieu of Maria's life. Indeed, I sensed active distaste on his part.

Acting as a go-between for all this was a young civil servant, Secretary to the inquiry, of the 'high-flyer' stream who attended all the sessions and played an important role. Relationships between the Chair and I were just possible whilst the inquiry was sitting, but broke down once drafting began, so it eventually fell to the Secretary to tell me, with tact and style, what the Chair thought about my suggestions! ('Dear Miss Stevenson, Mr Field-Fisher has asked me to tell you…') This was Christine Hallett, now retired Principal of Stirling University. I learned from her some of the skills of senior civil servants, including the writing of minutes.

Looking back and in the light of subsequent experiences, I am sure I would not have been so intractable, and ending up by writing a minority report, if I had worked with a Chair who had a better understanding and interest in the complex matters we were considering. (After all, I had survived the Supplementary Benefits Commission rather well.) This is a pity because I think that my views have not always been understood by subsequent readers or, more often, by those who have heard about them. My Minority Report has been interpreted as 'standing up for social work'. It is not generally known that I wrote the section on inter-agency working in the main report. It was not controversial but I suspect the Chair thought it was less important than I did.

In the Minority Report I dissociated myself from the analysis of the first part of Maria's life, culminating in her return to the care of her mother and stepfather. I did not dissent from the analysis of the last part of her life and of the terrible events which resulted in her death. The early story turned on the fact that Maria had been formally placed, in her infancy, as a foster child with an aunt, with a proviso that the aunt had been approved for the care of Maria only. The aunt was on bad terms with Maria's mother and there was conflicting evidence about the extent to which the mother had sought and been allowed to visit her daughter. It was pretty clear that Maria's aunt wanted this to be a 'quasi-adoption' and that, for whatever very mixed reasons, her mother did not. Thus, a key part of the analysis concerned the decision of the East Sussex Children's Department to allow Maria to return to the care of her mother, a decision of which the main report is unequivocally critical. Now this, of course, leads us into the territory which is the most contested in child welfare and in which battles rage to this day; matters concerning 'permanence', parental rights, the rights of the child, and so on. I suspect that if I had been able to discuss the complexities of these matters with the Chair and they could have been reflected in the Majority Report, there would have been no need to write the Minority Report.

In fact, more than thirty years afterwards, I am more comfortable with what I wrote about inter-agency and inter-professional working, simplistic though some of it must seem to today's readers.

After the long wrangles over the report were over, it was finally published in 1974. Apart from a formal letter of thanks (drafted by our secretary, Christine Hallett!), I had no official reactions to it. I was hurt and baffled that the Chief Social Work Inspector (from which the invitation had initially come over the phone) did not communicate in any way. I still think there might have been a way to do so without breaching protocol.

The Impact of the Maria Colwell Inquiry

The consequences of the Maria Colwell inquiry have been huge, for me personally, but also for the future of child welfare in the UK. It marked the beginning of a journey for the protection of children, a recognition that cooperative activity was absolutely essential. I struggle to understand and convey the effect on my career and on child protection. Nothing until then, in my own practice or as a tutor, had focussed my attention on child abuse, even though as students, we were aware that the death of a foster child in 1945 (Dennis O'Neill) had been significant in the setting up of children's departments in 1948. Nigel Parton's analysis (1985) showed how British paediatricians in the 1950s were beginning to write of concerns about 'battered babies' emanating from the United States. This put the Maria Colwell inquiry into a social and historical perspective. We were seeing the emergence of a major social anxiety (some suggested 'moral panic') which was to cloud the skies of British child welfare for the next 35 years, probably more.

As a result of the Maria Colwell inquiry, there were many invitations to speak to professional audiences. From these encounters, three essential themes became clear to me. First, the deeply contentious issue of a child's separation from the parents and of their placements (at what age, with whom and with what contact) arouses passions and primitive emotions which affect us all, even those who are knowledgeable and sophisticated in such matters. Second, it is inevitable that some of these feelings will be projected onto the social workers who carry the main responsibility for these decisions. Third, the Maria Colwell inquiry contributed to a much more serious examination than hitherto of the part played by other agencies and professionals in the protection of children. Successive governments have built on that through the development of inter-agency guidance in relation to the protection of children.

It is difficult to describe the immediate personal impact of participation in such inquiries. A concentration on the detail of the life of a child, fuelled by a forensic insistence on accuracy of every episode creates a kind of obsessiveness; it is hard to think or talk of anything else. One is in danger of becoming a bore the longer it goes on. It may well be that this is, in part, a protective mechanism since it focuses on intellectual understanding rather than emotional reactions to what are usually tragic and disturbing events. Making sense (or trying to) of awfulness is a help. People have asked me, 'Did you not feel dreadfully distressed by what you heard?' It is easier to agree but it is not entirely true. Perhaps it is because it is more bearable when *there is a job to be done*. There were deep, sad feelings but I cannot remember crying at any time during those weeks and months. I do recall one event which could have been a step too far and which is symptomatic of the confusion there was about the nature of evidence for such inquiries. We were asked if we wished to see the videos of the autopsy carried out on Maria (by this time the stepfather was in prison). I had a bad moment wondering whether the Chair (a criminal lawyer) would want to do so and was greatly relieved when he declined, although with some hesitation.

After the inquiry, I felt flat and empty, possibly depressed but certainly exhausted. I felt quite bewildered and ambivalent when my former boss, Kenneth Brill, who was by then Secretary of the British Association of Social Workers, gave me, on behalf of the

Association, a leather bound copy of the original report, in its unpublished form, with a laudatory inscription.

I recall feeling more embarrassment, surprise and unease than pleasure at this tribute. The word 'brilliant' was to me inappropriate and the phrase 'humble tribute' came, strangely, from the man who had seen me at my most naïve (as a Care Assistant of eighteen in a children's home) and later as a gaffe-prone, novice Child Care Officer. I could not connect the word 'brilliant' with my contribution to a report of this kind. As for 'courageous' this had never occurred to me because, at this time, I felt that there was nothing else I could do but dissent from the blinkered approach (as I saw it) of the Chair.

At that time, I had no idea how deeply the resistance to minority reports in such documents is embedded in the British political psyche. The reaching of consensus was somehow the 'greater good' which may be why the senior officials at the commissioning body, the DHSS, could not handle me sensibly afterwards! I was forewarned when, ten years later, I strayed again into the field of minority reports as a member of The Royal Commission on Civil Liability & Compensation for Personal Injury (The Pearson Commission) in 1978.

The Colwell Inquiry has affected the rest of my career in all sorts of ways and at different levels. It gave me a kind of celebrity status but in ways which were very uncomfortable. I did not want to be seen as a defender of social work 'right or wrong' and, indeed, nothing of what I wrote in the report can be thus described. My frustration (which continues) was that the value of social work and its difficulties were not appreciated. Nor did I want my professional interests to be squeezed into one box – that of child abuse and protection. Indeed, I had welcomed the creation, in 1970, of Social Services Departments (SSDs) in place of fragmented services for families and embraced the idea of generic training for social workers with enthusiasm. Inevitably, however, my position following the Colwell inquiry meant that work came my way (research, lectures, serious case reviews, etc.) which focussed attention on this field.

Throughout my career I have 'broken out' in various ways; most importantly in making links between child and adult abuse and (latterly) in examining the harmful effects of serious neglect, both of children and vulnerable adults. But over forty years, issues concerning child maltreatment have been very significant in my professional life; not least were the years immediately after formal retirement when I chaired a number of Area Child Protection Committees (now Local Safeguarding Children Boards).

9

Unresolved Issues for
Social Work

Much of what I have said about my working life has focused on child welfare. As I have pointed out in this memoir, especially due to my involvement in the Maria Colwell inquiry my professional identity has been very publicly identified with child protection matters. But there is more to the story. In the 1980s I made a considered decision to develop research and teaching interests in ageing, in particular in the needs of vulnerable and frail very old people. My motivations for developing my work in this direction are explained in depth in the 1999 Graham Lecture, reproduced in Appendix II of this memoir. There I mention how I can trace a theme to when, as a student with the Family Welfare Association, I had grieved over 'Percy', an old man living in a basement in Paddington. He was utterly alone. I, young and foolish, promised to keep in touch with him and did not do so. It remains for me a particularly poignant aspect of the lives of some very old people that they are emotionally or physically alone in their last years. In the early 1980s I was invited to become Chair of Age Concern

---

Olive's ill-health prevented her from completing her work on this chapter. Professor Harry Ferguson has drawn together the themes of Olive's argument and, building on previously published work in Bower (2005), has provided a concluding section for the chapter.

England. A whole new world opened up to me, which has never closed down. The significance of those years was epitomised by my choice of topic 'Women in Old Age' for my inaugural lecture at Nottingham University in 1986. As this work continued into the 1990s I began to join up thoughts on child protection with the protection of very old people from abuse. While the analysis on key issues in social work that follows in this chapter is focused on child protection, the dilemmas and challenges raised also apply to social work's role in promoting the welfare and protection of vulnerable adults. The core issue is how are we to create social work organisations and practices that are compassionate in their encounters with those who are suffering in poverty and from other forms of social injustice and that ensure social workers have the personal qualities, training, insight and support to be emotionally attuned to the lives of children and adults and to their own needs as human beings and professionals.

Looking back, how do I now see the ongoing, harsh, contentious and unresolved debates about child protection?

There are two strands in this. One is about social work itself. The other concerns the complex interactions between various agencies and professionals which is required for effective child protection practice. So far as social work is concerned, I did not see clearly that what I believed (and still do) were the essential ingredients of good social work in child protection were being submerged and distorted by social forces and trends, some largely outside my control but others which I had myself supported. I now see that the 1970s and early 1980s were the period in which social work took (or was taken down) wrong turnings. Among the many issues, three stand out for me: the consequences of the creation of Social Services Departments; the way in which qualifying training developed; and the decision by the British Association of Social Workers (BASW) that social workers need not be qualified to be members of the association.

Wrong Turnings

The creation of Social Services Departments, although well intentioned, was not adequately supported by central government in terms of resources, above all in terms of staff training. The result was that the dream of social policy analysts was never translated into the gritty reality of equipping social workers adequately for new roles or of developing specialisms *within* genericism which were formally sanctioned and resourced. Instead, in some places, there was an ideological flight to 'patchism', an appealing, anti-elitist model of social work which emphasised locality and community-focussed activity with minimal emphasis on the worker as carrying legal authority. SSDs muddled through, quite unprepared for the succession of calamities and increasing frequency of inquiries into child deaths. So, I am left with the uncomfortable awareness that I did not see what was happening. Indeed, it may be that during my time with the Supplementary Benefits Commission – something quite other – I took my eye off the ball and was then swept away with the attractive idea that a simple reorganisation of services could put the model of generic qualifying training into practice.

My resistance to facing the difficulties associated with genericism is epitomised by my (private) reaction to an article by Joan Vann in the *British Journal of Social Work* (1971) at the time I was editor. It was an excellent piece, written with the head and the heart, warning of what might be lost to child care through the Seebohm reorganisations, in terms of a skilled workforce and the transmission of practice wisdom. All these years later, it remains in my mind as *something I did not want to read.* (Happily, my editorial integrity was not affected. It was published.)

Another matter about which I feel I was blinkered was on my own doorstep. The Central Council for Education and Training in Social Work (CCETSW) had been formed in 1971. The policy logic of this development seemed inexorable. Social work, from its earliest days as a response to poverty, had developed a range of agencies tailored to specific needs and problems in the years before the Second World War. Thus, 'almoners' – later medical social workers – in hospitals, more specialised psychiatric social workers in mental hospitals, probation officers to serve the courts; all had evolved distinct identities. The raft of Welfare State legislation at the end of the War freed social workers, to an extent, from some of the issues of poverty, notably in relation to the costs of healthcare.

The rise of the child care service from 1948 marked a further shift from a 'poverty-centric' occupation to one for which there was a legislative intention to provide care as well as could be expected of a 'good parent'. (How sad that all sounds now.) Thus, during the 1960s, British social work was freed, to an extent, from the task of alleviating the grosser aspects of poverty, and attracted increasing numbers of well-educated (mostly) women with a strong social awareness. (This was in part the result of wartime experience.) It became easier to see what the different kinds of social work had in common. This phase can be seen as the emergence in the 1960s and 1970s of a profession, not dissimilar to the emergence of the profession of medicine in which a variety of specialisms (including the once completely separate surgery) claimed a hugely significant place in western societies.

I will examine further these issues concerning how social work has developed into the present by considering the contributions of three influential figures in the development of social work. In these post-war years, British social work was profoundly affected by the United States. We who considered ourselves progressive were ready for change, looking to models and theories upon which to base the next stage of our development. This was symbolised by the emergence of Eileen Younghusband as a major national figure from the years 1950 to 1980.

Eileen Younghusband

Eileen Younghusband (later Dame), born in 1902, was a remarkable woman. The daughter of Major Sir Francis Younghusband, she was brought up in aristocratic circles. She commanded respect with a laconic manner, high intelligence and dry wit. She became, in the 1960s and 1970s, a key influence both in the rapid expansion of social work training, including two year non-graduate courses, and in the more 'generic' education of social workers.

She had close contact with leaders of social work in the United States, some of whose enthusiasm for various forms of psychoanalytic theory for social case workers became well known to social workers and social work teachers in the UK, for example, Charlotte Towle, Florence Hollis, Felix P. Biestek, Helen Perlman and Harriet Bartlett. At a time when British literature for social workers was scant, it was journal articles and books by these authors that found their way onto our shelves.

The late Kathleen Jones, in an undervalued biography of Eileen Younghusband (1984), shows her as possessing many of the fine qualities of nineteenth-century social reformers. Maybe she was born a bit too late. She was brought up in India and England with the privileges and deprivations that are associated with that background. A beloved Nanny provided her early care and her departure was traumatic; a second Nanny, known only as 'Shortie' because Eileen refused to call another person Nanny, also became beloved. Her mother floated about in big hats. University education was regarded as unsuitable, despite evidence of her abilities. She did not get this opportunity until she was 27 when she went to the LSE for three years, gaining a diploma and degree in social studies.

The biography reveals that Younghusband worked against the grain of class assumptions for the role of women; she had little interest in being married and was fired by ideas and learning. In fact, her childhood education, at home with tutors, gave her an excellent grounding. She was profoundly concerned about hardship and poverty and spent much time in those bastions of early social work – the university settlements in London. I well recall my sense of unease and rejection of those phenomena when I was a student in the 1950s. They were the past and we were the future. I was in my twenties and Eileen was fifty. She was not a qualified social worker; there were fewer opportunities then to become a social worker. Her outstanding intellectual capacity made it natural that she should seek models and theories to understand and shape the processes of social work.

Eileen Younghusband did not publish a great deal, although her influence was present in much of the discourse and planning for social work in the period. Much of her writing is dry, to the point of being emotionally dead but in the opening of her substantial book, *Social Work in Britain: 1950–1975*, published in 1978, she puts her finger on the social work dilemma that is with us today. She wrote:

> This is a story full of tensions, of unrecorded achievement in the lives of individual people, of blind spots and irrelevant intervention or of the little that was sometimes enough. It is also the story of a profession's struggles to understand many different kinds of people better in their family and social circumstances or sudden crises... *this included a fitfully recognised need to combine practical help with understanding of human behaviour'.* [My italics.]
>
> (Eileen Younghusband, 1978, p.1)

This is an eloquent and heartfelt passage. It is not fanciful to see this journey of exploration as a search to understand better both the causes of and remedies for social injustice and inequality, but also a search for the best ways of easing the pain of deprivation and frustration, both of which she endured.

Social Work in Britain, for some reason which I do not fully understand, attracted very little attention. Perhaps it was because the detailed and descriptive accounts of the major controversies of the time were given with an air of detachment. They do not capture the intensity of the views current at the time she was writing.

The pity of all this is that Eileen Younghusband turned to the American social workers for theoretical frameworks and it was their literature which dominated the early days of generic training at the LSE. Our own literature, of course, was sparse by comparison. But it seems that Eileen made little contribution to the development of indigenous writing about social work. For example, I did not have any contact with her when I was the first editor of the *British Journal of Social Work*. Nor did I find any reference in Kathleen Jones' biography to her having had any productive contact with Clare Winnicott whose writing was so important to the development of British child welfare. There was a bitter falling out at the LSE over course content and governance in the early 1960s and Eileen withdrew, deeply upset. She later became a 'doyenne' in the International Society of Social Work (ISSW) movement.

So, what am I trying to say? There is a sadness about Eileen Younghusband's life and works in relation to the development of English social work. A woman of formidable intellect, principled and committed, devoted daughter and good friend, she assumed positions of great significance in those critical post-war years. She had the capacity to shape ideas into realities; the National Institute of Social Work being one, structures for the expansion of social work training being another; the list goes on. But, somehow, she did not manage to relate her plans for English social work to home-grown attitudes and behaviours and had, perhaps, too little awareness of the impact of her class and personality.

Clare Winnicott & the Role of the Social Worker

I was caught up in all of these controversies; it was a dominant motif in the 1960s and 1970s (see my article in the *British Journal of Social Work*, 1971). There are two strands. The first concerns the idea of genericism in social work training which paralleled the structural changes, the introduction of Social Services Departments (SSDs) which were to begin in 1970. The idea of a unified profession appealed to me greatly. In all honesty, I expect that the idea of increased power and status was attractive. But I do not think that my motives were mainly about professional power. I was struggling to find a model which described what claim social work had to distinctiveness. It ran something like this:

> Social work seeks to help individuals, family and communities who have difficulties in their relationships resulting in conflicts and deprivations. A social worker moves between the inner and outer worlds of the person(s) they are seeking to help; that is, they may focus on the feelings, attitudes etc. of the person(s) or on the adverse social circumstances in which such person(s) exist, or, most likely, both. They are not either psychotherapists or social reformers (except indirectly) but employ some of the attributes (but not the depth of expertise) of both.

This approach to understanding the role of the social worker owes much to Clare Winnicott. In fact, it is only relatively recently, in re-reading Clare's work in preparation for this book that I came to realise that I had internalised so much of her teaching that it became my own. This raises fascinating questions about the nature of deep plagiarism such as that musical composers are often accused of.

In 2009, I gave a lecture on the relevance of Clare Winnicott's ideas on social work with children, in today's context. (See Appendix I of this volume for the text of this previously unpublished lecture.) In the process of doing so, I realised the extent of my uneasiness about my relationship with Clare in later years. That was due, in no small measure, to a sense that I had betrayed her in not offering effective support after she returned to the LSE in the mid-1970s following her husband Donald's death in 1971. Clare's contribution has been well described by Kanter (2004).

In 1975, the LSE faculty was in ferment and the splits between academics deep and unbridgeable, highlighted by the appointment of an American expert in community development. As Kanter (2004) points out, the LSE battles were a microcosm for the 'soul of social work'. To whom did it belong? The inner or the outer worlds? Either those drawn by psychoanalytic thought or more politically motivated community developers. There was no possibility of arguing that it was both. And Clare was in no state to manage it. Her grief was profound; she had, of course, lost her partner in work and intellectual life as well as in love, and the LSE milieu must have seemed totally alien at that time. It is not surprising that she turned away from social work and I have no illusions that I could have done anything to alter that. But I know in my heart that my professional preoccupations, and my difficulty in engaging with her in debates about the 'soul of social work' led to a distance between us (never explicit) which I deeply regret.

Barbara Wootton

The emerging claims of social work as a distinctive profession stirred up hornets' nests during the 1970s – and they did feel like hornets' nests at the time – for our aspirations coincided with the rise of a group of able and angry sociologists whose critique of social class and poverty was fierce. They deplored the negative aspects of professional power with its claims to expertise and consequent 'nest feathering'. Here were social workers (one group was described by Handler as 'coercive Children's Officers') trying to grab occupational respectability, and, by a sneaky route, taking unto themselves some of the power of psychoanalysis. Such sentiments began to find expression in the birth of 'Radical Social Work' and the book by Bailey and Brake (1975) of that title.

A further 'hornet sting' came from the formidable Barbara Wootton (later Baroness), an eminent economist who held a chair at Royal Holloway College in London. In 1959, when I was in my fifth year as a qualified social worker and at the Tavistock Clinic, Wootton published *Social Science and Social Pathology*. She devoted a long chapter to an analysis of social work in Britain at the time. It is notable that she considered this important enough to include in her scholarly and far-reaching book. In this chapter, she argued that social work has taken a wrong turning away from the alleviation of social and material problems towards a preoccupation with the inner worlds of clients, borrowing (pretentiously, she argues) from psychoanalytic theory. She refers to extensive borrowing from American social work education and is scathing about Eileen Younghusband's part in influencing British social work.

Re-reading this chapter after fifty years, it still remains an unsettling and rather infuriating experience! It is well written and trenchant; it raises extremely important questions about the role of social work; it rightly exposes ludicrously pretentious statements by some who tried to emulate psychoanalysis. And yet, it was just plain wrong as a description of the vast majority of British social work activity. In fact, there were many rather fumbling attempts at delineating a range of theories for social work, sometimes leaving students 'not waving but drowning', and little evidence of those translated in any meaningful way into mainstream practice. My own research, published in *Social Service Teams – the Practitioner's View* (1978), strongly confirmed that.

Wootton does not refer to Clare Winnicott, who had, by 1959, begun to contribute significantly to the British social work literature. Had she done so, she would have seen the clear and unequivocal distinctions which she made between the role of social workers in children's services and the psychotherapist. But she would also have seen a powerful case for the utilisation of aspects of psychoanalytic theory in understanding and attempting to help deprived children and those who seek to help them, presented by Clare in admirably simple, jargon-free language. So, Wootton refused to acknowledge that 'moving between inner and outer worlds' is integral to social work and by her caustic wit contributed to the persisting difficulties in exploring the dynamics of that movement. This was followed by other writers, some much less able. Some were in full retreat from an uncomfortable inner reality, some in academic life, anxious about competition from a new group in their midst such Colin Brewer and June Lait (1980). Some, who were Marxists, held political views that excluded considerations of the inner world (Corrigan & Leonard, 1978).

I was never in doubt that the essence of social work skill lay in some combination of reflective and practical work with and for the person in need of help. The balance between the two varies greatly according to the individual and their circumstances. However, I much regret that in those years (1970–1990), I was so preoccupied with a range of social, professional and educational issues, that the Wootton critique (to put it crudely) was not centre stage in my mind. In the years from 1954 to 1974, the influence of psychoanalytic thinking, in which the Winnicotts played a significant part, underpinned a great deal of my practice, my teaching and my writing. After that I was pulled in various directions, all interesting and exciting, but I can see now that I took my eye off the ball. I did not recognise that social work, especially in statutory children's services, was going badly wrong and this was in part because crucial issues about relationships with children and families were not well enough understood.

We are now in an era when we scarcely recognise psychoanalytic ways of understanding behaviour and interaction. This was brought home to me forcibly when I contributed a Foreword to *Psychoanalytic Theory for Social Work Practice: Thinking under Fire* (Bower, 2005). In it, I commented that there were three assumptions, derived from psychoanalytic theory, which were indispensible to good practice. These are:

1 Past experiences affect current attitudes and behaviour.
2 We are not always consciously aware of the ways in which past experience affects behaviour.
3 Clients may have feelings about the worker (and vice versa) that derive from other (sometimes unconscious) unconnected experience.

The first two of these are now pretty well self-evident and no longer contentious. Even the third does not come as a shock, especially when the words 'transference' and 'counter-transference' do not creep in and create anxiety! Well-worn as these ideas are, I have been shocked to find how little such basic concepts are utilised in everyday processes of supervision and discussion.

What Now Needs to be Done?

The first area in need of change and development concerns the context within which social workers are educated. I would like to think that we have come far enough to accept that the ideological battles, fascinating and important as they are, should not, and need not, divert us from the sensible use of psychoanalytic theories and providing students and qualified social workers with an understanding of the importance of 'moving between inner and outer worlds' as one important element in the development of the skills of social work. If we cannot move forward on this, from what theory are our students going to try and understand some of the most complex feelings and actions of their clients? Without such an attempt, intervention to improve their lot is unguided. Furthermore, workers' awareness of their own reactions will be inadequate. Thus I am arguing for a way of examining peoples' behaviour which takes us 'a layer down'. This is not always necessary or appropriate; for example the widespread use of cognitive behavioural techniques in certain kinds of emotional disturbance is demonstrably valuable. However, it is my contention that this type of approach is not adequate for many of the situations in which a worker in social work routinely finds his- or herself.

The second area where change needs to happen lies in agencies. It is useless to promote an approach to theory which involves reflection and the raising of awareness of the self and others, unless the host agency respects its importance and facilitates its development. This is a huge agenda, at first sight very daunting. What we have to think about is how to create a climate and culture which allows this way of thinking to flourish. Much used words like 'space' and 'reflection' immediately suggest 'time' to the managerially challenged. But we have reached a point where it must be acknowledged that time needs to be used differently if the goal of better practice (and fewer disasters) is to be met. Organisational life must be reconfigured to enable social workers to have the time, knowledge, skills and confidence to work creatively and freely with children and parents.

Of particular significance in changing organisational culture is the use of supervision as a tool for performance development, not simply for managerial control (I do not dispute the need for the latter). It may be that these two elements in supervision could be separated. For example, work which I undertook in one local authority suggested the possibility of increased peer group consultation for experienced workers, with focused case discussion at its heart. Tailored plans for individual development are also essential. A further way of introducing these reflective processes is through interprofessional case-focused meetings, with facilitation, an approach I have seen being very successfully achieved in relation to cases of serious neglect (Glennie et al, 1998).

A changed style of working must be underpinned by the use of concepts and theories designed better to understand what is happening to workers and their clients. There has been much talk about 'evidence based practice' in recent years. It is crucial however that we are clear as to what we consider to be 'evidence'. Those who believe as I do that there are substantial aspects of psychoanalytic theory and the impact of practice that moves between inner and outer worlds which can be 'evidenced', must be prepared to make explicit their grounds for so believing. In offering reflections on my life and what I have learned during a sixty-year career in social work, I hope that this book will make a contribution to improving social work, re-energising its work force and enhancing the lives of the vulnerable people it exists to serve.

References

Bailey R. & Brake M. (1975), *Radical Social Work*, Edward Arnold: London.

Bower M. (2005), *Psychoanalytic Theory for Social Work Practice: Thinking Under Fire*, Routledge: London.

Bowlby J. (1997), *Attachment & Loss*, Volume 1, (revised edition), Pimlico: London.

Brewer C. & Lait J. (1980), *Can Social Work Survive?* Maurice Temple Smith: London.

Corrigan P. & Leonard P. (1978), *Social Work Practice Under Capitalism: A Marxist Approach*, Macmillan: London.

Department of Health and Social Security (1988), *Child Abuse in Cleveland 1987: Inquiry Report*, HMSO: London.

Department of Health and Social Security (2003), *The Victoria Climbié Inquiry*, HMSO: London.

Durrell L. (1985), 'Clouds of Glory', *Collected Poems 1931–1974*, Faber & Faber: London.

Glennie S., Cruden B. & Thorn J. (1998), *Neglected Children: Maintaining Hope, Optimism and Direction*, Notts County and City Child Protection Committees.

Jones K. (1984), *Eileen Younghusband: A Biography*, Bedford Square Press: London.

Kanter J. (2004), *Face to Face with Children: The Life & Work of Clare Winnicott*, Karnac Books: London.

Lee L. (1959/1970), *Cider with Rosie*, Penguin: London.

Mattinson J. (1970), *Marriage and Mental Handicap*, Duckworth: London.

Parsloe P. *et al* (1978), *Social Service Teams – the Practitioner's View*, HMSO: London.

Parton N. (1985), *The Politics of Child Abuse*, Palgrave Macmillan: London.

Pearson Commission (established 1973, report 1978), *Royal Commission on Civil Liability & Compensation for Personal Injury*.

Robertson J. & Robertson J. (1952), 'A Two-Year-Old Goes to Hospital', Concorde Film Council: Ipswich.

Stevenson O. (1964/1977), *Someone Else's Child*, 2nd edn, Routledge & Kegan Paul: London.

Stevenson O. (1971), 'Knowledge for Social Work', *British Journal of Social Work*, (1)2.

Stevenson O. (1972), *Claimant or Client? A social worker's view of the Supplementary Benefits Commission*, Allen & Unwin: London.

Stevenson O. (2005), 'Foreword' in Bower M. (ed.), *Psychoanalytic Theory for Social Work Practice: Thinking under Fire*, Routledge: Abingdon.

Tawney R.H. (2006), *Religion and the Rise of Capitalism*, Read Books.

Tawney R.H. (2010), *The Acquisitive Society*, Forgotten Books.

Tillich P. (1960), *Love, Power and Justice*, Oxford University Press Inc: New York.

Vann J. (1971), 'The Child as a Client of the Social Services Department: Some Implications for the Training of Social Workers', *British Journal of Social Work*, 1 (2) pp.209–24.

Wittenberg-Salzberger I. (1970), *Psychoanalytic Insight and Relationships: A Kleinian Approach*, Routledge: London.

Wootton B. (1959), *Social Science and Social Pathology*, Allen & Unwin: London.

Younghusband E. (1978), *Social Work in Britain: 1950–1975: a follow-up study* vol.2, Allen & Unwin: London.

APPENDIX I

Direct Work with Children
The Relevance of Clare Winnicott's Teaching to Contemporary Social Work Practice

As I write this, I am looking at the photograph of Clare Winnicott on the front of her biography (Kanter, 2004). My memory of her is crystal clear; fair hair, green eyes, lovely (and expensive!) clothes; direct, sometimes uncomfortably so; feisty; a very good listener – so actively attentive; teaching from the bottom of her mind, seeking always to communicate effectively; entering into the moment fully and creatively, whether in party spirit or in serious mode.

And what of context? We are talking about the post-war years; I was her student in 1953 at the LSE. They were not only post-war years, with their raft of 'welfare state' legislation; they were also the post-evacuation years, when thousands of children had been sent out of London and other big cities, for their physical safety but with little understanding of the emotional consequences. For years, there has been little professional or academic interest in the story of the

---

This lecture on the relevance of Clare Winnicott's teaching to contemporary social work practice was given at Nottingham University in September 2009.

evacuated children within the UK. This is in contrast to coverage of the Jewish children who came here on the 'Kindertransport' or that concerning children sent from here to Australia and Canada in the post-war years.

Clare, a psychiatric social worker and her future husband Donald, a paediatrician and psychoanalyst, had been deeply involved in the care of those evacuated children, including, and especially, those who had proved 'unfosterable' and ended up in 'hostels'. They worked in Oxfordshire, offering advice, support and consultation. Clare's teaching therefore, was rooted in concern for children who had had disrupted lives and, often, problematic relations with their parents. This was in direct contrast to some of the work of the (then) Child Guidance Clinics, whose clientele tended to be drawn from intact families in which children were displaying behavioural difficulties. Clare pioneered a 'Child Care Course' (there were only three to begin with) for graduate students, which had at its heart the children whose needs and problems fell under the new Children Act 1948. This was expressly designed to provide unified departments, within local government, for children who were, or might be, deprived of an ordinary home life because of parental difficulties.

Evacuation had brought to the attention of the country not only the extent of the poverty in which so many children had lived, but also the dire effects of separation and trauma. Nor were the alternatives to the family problem-free. Pre-war arrangements for residential and foster care were seen to be inadequate and a particular scandal, a child Dennis O'Neill, killed by foster parents in 1947, was widely discussed in the serious papers.

During the immediate post-war period, running in parallel with the trends I have been describing, the work of John Bowlby on attachment, linked in the first instance to delinquent children (Bowlby, [1944] 1997), was taking shape. The early films of James and Joyce Robertson built on these foundations and offered compelling evidence of the effects on young children of separation from parents (Robertson, 1952).

Last year, I saw the 1953 film again, after many years, at a conference of paediatricians. I was reminded of the huge significance of that film, and those who backed it, in changing hospital practice so that mothers could be admitted with their young children. I also noted that I remembered it so well, wincing in advance of distressing shots of Laura in her cot.

I am sketching in here the focus of those early years in children's services, which were on children in transit, or in limbo when they should have been at least in transit.

Clare Winnicott believed that social work, an emerging profession, was critical to the provision of a child care service which would help the child within his/her environment. By that, she meant that social workers had a job to do both with the child directly and for the child. Most of this paper is about the former – the direct work; but she never forgot that the social work role is not simply helping a child to adjust. It is also about influencing the environment in which the developing child grows up. That environment usually, but not exclusively, is about the people directly involved with the child. (Of course, sometimes those people may only be in the child's head at a given time; a kind of virtual reality rather than reality.)

I am emphasising this because it is a distortion of Clare's 'message' to suggest it was all about what is in the head/heart of the child, important as that is. Clare's social work was also rooted in practical activity which was, however, always connected to another kind of reality – children's feelings. She confronted fearlessly chief education officers, or any administrator whom she believed was preventing the execution of the right care plan for a child. She was secure in her professionalism.

Those of you who have read her biography (Kanter, 2004) will understand why I stress these points. Starting as a social worker she became a psychoanalyst and this came to be used, quite unjustifiably, as a kind of stick to beat her with, and, by association, child care social work as it struggled to come of age. This is a complex story, too long to be told here, some of which is about the influence of American social work, never of particular interest to Clare. It has, however, long-term consequences relevant to our theme today. Afraid of becoming mini-psychoanalysts, some social workers proceeded to throw the baby out with the bath-water (yes, I know, an unfortunate image); they retreated from seeking to understand children's feelings about their situation.

There are curious contradictions about this. The rise of the idea of the 'life story book' for children in foster and adoptive care points to a contrary trend. This level of work with a child suggests a recognition of the child's needs to make sense of the jigsaw puzzle of his or her life. Surely this must mean helping children to understand their feelings about it all? When done well in that context, it obviously requires the social worker to empathise and help the child to verbalise his or her feelings. But it is one of the many confusing and worrying aspects of contemporary practice that these skills have not, by and large, been carried across to other spheres of child care practice, noticeably in relation to children in their own homes who are neglected or maltreated. Hence, many Serious Case Reviews point to the failure of social workers to establish effective communication with children. Some underlying reasons for this have been discussed by Ferguson (2009), who cites the Jasmine Beckford Serious Case Review of 1985 as an example.

We are still paying the price today of that retreat from our responsibility to reach out and respond to children's feelings. The word 'therapeutic', which Clare pointed out nearly fifty years ago (1963 in Kanter 2004, p.170) only means 'tending to the cure of' and is still too readily conflated with '*psycho*therapeutic' when we discuss helping children through play.

There were other factors in addition to confusion over psychoanalytic theory that drew social workers away from the development of their skills in working directly with children. And, before turning to the relevance of Clare's teaching to practice today, I need to acknowledge the part that I, and others of my generation, played in allowing her wisdom to be pushed into the background. It was Clare's misfortune that too soon after she weighed into the battle for improved children's services and pinned her hopes to the emerging cadre of social workers, other forces came into play, professional and political. The crucial professional one was, of course, the emergence of the concept of generic social work, from the United States, much affected by the influential and rather intimidating figure of Dame Eileen Younghusband, who played a major part in the generic model which we (to an extent) imported from the United States and in the huge expansion of social work in the 1960s. There are 'tides in the affairs of men' and this tide proved irresistible. I was caught up in the excitement of the idea that social work could be conceived as a coherent whole, with underlying values, theories and skills which could be transferred to all user (client) groups. Lacking literature of our own, our ideas were fed by powerful and able figures, mostly women, on the American scene. In England and Wales there was a rare confluence of interests; academic, (new, 'generic' courses), administrative ('Seebohm departments'), and quasi-professional (the creation of the British Association of Social Workers) from separate organisations, such as the Association of Child Care Officers and the Institute of Medical Social Workers. Then, in 1980, the generic seal was set by the creation of the Central Council for Education and Training in Social Work, which unified social work training nationally and began to develop national requirements. All of this, at the time seemed progressive and worthwhile; in retrospect it is easy to see how unprepared society, government and social work academia were for this very large undertaking.

This is a subject of another lecture. What I must say, however, is that it has taken me many years to bring to the surface the nagging sense of my disloyalty to Clare and my guilt that I went along too readily with the current trends. I recall that in 1970, when I was editor of the new *British Journal of Social Work* I accepted an article by Joan Vann in which she raised her fears for the child care service in the new 'generic' context. I recognised the article as well written and important and published it, but I simply did not want to heed its warning. It was simply too painful. I am not so omnipotent as to think that I could have significantly affected policy and practice in those years. But I did not let myself see the dangers ahead. Not did I manage well the tension in myself between my loyalty and admiration for Clare and what she stood for, and the forces for change which were attractive but which, to be blunt, resulted in a weakening of the child care service in its early and vulnerable days.

Overcrowded curricula and other preoccupations squeezed out many of the early 'child-centred' initiatives on courses. There was very little development of direct work with children in the 1970s and 1980s within social service departments except in aspects of fostering and adoption. Ironically, this was the time when the abuse of children in their families began to hit the headlines and when practice skills in handling such situations were desperately needed. Kanter, in his biography (2004), cites the late Lucy Faithfull 'recalling Clare's despair about British social work in the last weeks before her death' in 1984 (p.151). These words affect me deeply.

Clare did not write specifically about child abuse or child protection, these words are not indexed in her published papers and I do not recall her ever teaching about it, although she gave expert witness at the Maria Colwell inquiry in 1973. What is clear, however, is that she was quite unafraid of the ideas which lie behind the word 'abuse', which replaced the naïve term 'battering' of the early 1970s. She and Donald were able to face the darkest parts of themselves and hence of other people. There was absolutely no sentimentality. Therefore her key ideas of good practice are all embedded in a background of understanding of the love, hate, joy, pain, sorrow, depression and passion which children experience.

Those of you who have read Kanter's biography will know that the personal and professional partnership of Donald and Clare Winnicott was exceptionally fruitful. Each was an independent spirit who brought to the partnership experience and creativity which was quite distinct. But the lasting value of their contribution to social work theory and practice was in part due to the ways they exchanged their thoughts and ideas, sometimes reframing them as they went along. Donald, I think, initiated more but Clare only used ideas in talking to social workers which she had fully internalised, and for which she could see the application in practice. Because of this, it is pointless to separate their contributions. Next month, I am giving a paper in London on Donald Winnicott's views on 'the anti-social tendency' in young people. Recently, I went to see a very old friend, now in her late eighties, who did the Psychiatric Social Work course at the LSE in the late 1970s, long after my time there. She is now blind and very deaf and tires easily. But she was reenergised when I referred to Donald, remembering his weekly teaching and how exactly it was, particularly in the sense of freedom and flexibility in practice which he conveyed. I went home. The next day she rang me and said 'I forgot to tell you something. He used to sit on the floor sometimes and show us how he communicated with children through "squiggles" in drawing. [Squiggles were games played when Donald and the child exchanged rough drawings and told each other about them.] And he said "This is what social workers do with children".' By this, he meant, I think, a direct attempt, through the medium of a simple frame, to understand how the child is feeling *at this time*.

Before I return to Clare's writing, let me pause to mention two aspects of Donald's work on anti-social children that seem to me of particular significance to my theme today. He suggested that many anti-social acts (he mentions stealing and destructiveness) are in fact indications of hope, a kind of shorthand, a cry for love and attention. In a moving passage, he wrote, 'Over and over again, one sees the moment of hope wasted or withered because of mismanagement or intolerance' (Winnicott, 1953). He links this argument to a distinction between the concepts of *privation* and *de*privation. The '*prived* child' is hopeless; he or she has never had 'good enough' experiences to mourn their loss. The *de*prived child wants to recapture those times of 'good enough' experiences.

Now there is a huge amount to discuss about this. How does one distinguish between 'the prived' and 'the deprived'? What part does early experience play in the anti-social behaviour of the child and adolescent? When is a child really hopeless? (How do we know?) The point I want to emphasise is that in direct work with children, there may be precious opportunities to grasp the moment of hope, even when it is presented in singularly awkward and unattractive ways.

I thought about this as I read, in *The Guardian* of 4 September 2009, the account of two young Doncaster boys, sent to secure units for grave assaults on two of their peers. A neighbour on the estate in which they lived was reported as saying, of the boys' wild and destructive behaviour, 'All they wanted was a bit of sympathy – a bit of love from their parents … For them to get into trouble … [meant] … that they were getting attention from their parents'. Of the younger boy (then only 10), she said he was '… crying out for attention from his mother and stepfather'.

The other idea from Donald which is useful here relates to his paper entitled 'Adolescence: Going Through the Doldrums' (1965). He writes of the need of the adolescent to find his or her own reality and that this may necessitate confrontation with the adults around him or her. The vital point, however, lies in the value of personal rather than institutional confrontation, i.e., in the context of relationships.

Clare contributed significantly to the understanding of communicating with children. Bogged down as we are in debates about 'assessment' (a word she did not use) her observations are relevant and salutary for us today.

She argued that we were not aiming at collecting information or taking a case history, although this may be important to our understanding and to help children ground their memories. Rather, she says, 'Our real aim is to keep children alive and to help them establish a sense of their own identity and worth in relation to other people. By keeping children alive, I am of course referring to maintaining their capacity to feel. If there are no feelings, there is no life, there is merely existence…' (1964 in Kanter 2004, p.187).

Behind this lies the profoundly important observation that any professional encounter with a child involves a relationship, however new or uncertain, and thus has therapeutic significance, for better or worse. The so-called 'objective observations' that one is required to make do not take place in an emotional vacuum. Even if I am only looking at a child, something is happening emotionally between us. If I actually feel nothing is happening, then that indeed is cause for worry about the child for, as Clare says, then '… there is no life, merely existence'. Unless, of course, it means we ourselves are not engaged!

I fear that administrative and bureaucratic demands sometimes blunt our sensibilities.

Once the essentially therapeutic nature of the encounter is accepted, then there are lots of questions about how this is to be achieved. Clare wrote about that. One of the better known of her comments arose directly from my invitation to her to speak at a conference in 1963 on the topic 'Face to Face with Children'. I still remember my feeling of embarrassment when she spoke at the conference of her discomfort with the title, which I had devised (though she acknowledged it was well meant!). She suggested that it conjured up a very definite picture of social worker and child confronting each other in an alarmingly direct way! 'The alarm', she added, 'would I am sure be shared at least equally by both parties' (1963 in Kanter 2004, pp.166–67). So if not eyeball to eyeball, how are these communications established?

Clearly, a natural path to communication is through play, an activity essential to human and much animal development. As early as 1945, Clare published a paper on 'children who cannot play'. Some of the illustrations were from the wartime experiences of traumatised children whose capacity to explore feelings in play had been stifled. She describes a six-year-old boy who was 'the most completely cut off child imaginable' (1945 in Kanter 2004, p.118). His parents had been killed in the air-raid shelter from which he had been rescued. He would not play when another child was around but gradually, after about eighteen months, began to do so whilst 'the foster mother sat knitting or reading'. Eventually he said suddenly, 'Does it hurt to get killed?' Clare speculates on the possibility that he could eventually ask the question because there was a foundation of 'good enough experiences with his parents' and he now felt safe with his foster carer, i.e., it was safe to go back. The profoundly important point which she makes is that play enables past experiences to be used and expressed in activities which the child takes on his or her own initiative (1945 in Kanter 2004, p.113). The child then can have a measure of control over the content of the play and what he or she draws from it.

I referred earlier to the fears of social workers that they were venturing into waters too deep when they engaged in 'therapeutic play'. It is time to leave these fears behind and recognise 'that play is a natural means of communication for all children and an essential tool in helping them clarify their feelings and thoughts' (1945 in Kanter 2004, p.113). In various places Clare deals, pretty trenchantly, with exaggerated fears of inappropriate 'psychotherapy' and says:

> A very simple and clear distinction can be made between psychotherapy and social work ... because of the nature of their work and the functions of their respective agencies ... The psychotherapist starts from the inside and is concerned with inner conflicts which hamper social development ...The social worker, on the other hand, starts off as a real person concerned with external events and people in the child's life ... In the course of her work with him, she will attempt to bridge the gap between the external world and his feelings about it and in so doing she will enter his inner world too. (1963 in Kanter 2004, p.171)

For us today, there are some worrying implications in that description of the social work role with children. In some localities there are dreadful difficulties in providing reasonable continuities of experience, when staff come and go. Nor is it always clear that the need in the child's life for 'a bridging person' is taken as a priority, when jobs are divided for administrative reasons or files go unread. Passing children around like parcels between workers to suit organisational models or difficulties would have sent Clare into a controlled rage.

I am sad when I hear that children are, more often than not, taken for parental 'contact' meetings by those who can drive but are neither 'bridges' for the children in the sense of 'knowing' about their world nor qualified to 'hear them' therapeutically. Taking children to places in cars was so pivotal in my own relationship with them that I cannot imagine the work without it. And it was wonderful we didn't have to look at each other! The recent article by Harry Ferguson (2009) to which I have already referred takes up the story.

Clare raises some specific issues about communication which merit special mention. One is the notion of symbols. 'A symbol is simply something that is allowed to stand for something else' (1964 in Kanter 2004, pp.184–85). More technically, a symbol is 'a secondary phenomenon which can be accepted and allowed to stand for a primary one', (temporarily or later permanently). She refers to the blanket or the woolly toy as examples of symbols which can give comfort and satisfaction to an infant or toddler. This familiar event was noted by Donald who developed explanatory theory around it; first described as 'transitional object', i.e., a kind of bridge between mother and infant, it was later called 'the first not-me possession' (Winnicott, 1953). It caught my imagination as a child-care student and became a dissertation topic! More important, it had a profound influence on my practice and, I am sure, on my fellow students. In those days, we received more children in care for short periods. The process included a careful inquiry about the 'bits of stuff' or battered soft toys to which the child was attached, so that they were not left behind on the journey to and fro. This small but very important action arose from a real understanding of the power of a symbol, in this case to provide 'the bridge' and to comfort. To me, it made sense of something I had observed before I did my LSE course. As an undergraduate I was working in a residential school for desperately disturbed children. Bedtimes were a huge source of tension; with scant regard for dental hygiene, some staff gave particular children a boiled sweet of a particular colour once they were in bed. So Ben, let's say, always had a purple one, even if the member of staff on duty differed. A symbol of some kind of continuity in fragmented lives, of people knowing and remembering what colour of sweet you liked.

Clare tackled head-on some reasons why we may be hesitant to engage directly with children. (She does not refer to simple 'awkwardness' and uncertainty, even shyness, yet this can be a factor. I well remember an essay by a male student in Nottingham about child observation which began: 'This was the first time I had ever met a person under three...') But Clare knew how powerful are the feelings in ourselves aroused by children, above all, those damaged or in distress, and how overwhelming these feelings may be to the worker. 'We are horrified at some of the experiences they have been through', she said, and continued: 'To work effectively with children, the first and most fundamental thing we have to know about is the strength of our own feelings about the suffering of children' (1963 in Kanter 2004, p.169).

These comments have assumed a particular poignancy in the context of child abuse tragedies over some forty years. Our Serious Case Reviews do not reveal what we could not bear to see. I have wondered in recent years why it has taken so long to place the issue of neglected children at the centre of child maltreatment concerns. A sense of impotence, of hopelessness in such cases (for complex reasons which I can't go into here) may have caused some workers to lift their emotional drawbridges, 'I can't face this; this child is in too much misery, cold, wet, dirty, hungry, alone'.

We ignore these hugely powerful feelings at our peril, and, of course, at the children's peril. But it should be an absolute duty of the organisations which employ social workers to ensure that there are safe places for these feelings to be explored and managed.

Clare did not, I think, ever envisage the extent to which social workers would be sucked into constraining rather than liberating bureaucracies. She wrote positively, not negatively, about being 'professional', not about elitism, gaining power and control, or feathering one's own nest – all criticisms of emerging child care social work in the 1960s and 1970s, often made by leather-jacketed sociologists. Rather, she wrote:

> Our professional relationship is in itself the basic technique … by means of which we relate ourselves to the individual and to the problem … Our professional self is the most highly organised and integrated part of ourselves. It is the best part of ourselves… we get reassurance about our value and goodness because people can take and use what we give. Our professional relationships are more balanced and reliable than our personal lives (1955 in Kanter 2004, pp.149–50).

I have found these words deeply helpful at various times, when other things fell apart. They also clearly acknowledge that some personal fulfilment is an acceptable component of a professional relationship, if it is properly directed. What Clare does not take up, though, is that there has to be a working context which facilitates such professional relationships. Hence, for example, my earlier criticism of arrangements for contact when the relevant social worker does not have the opportunity to be with the child. Or when pressure to complete assessments on time stifles the essentials in a therapeutic encounter. Her words remain with me as a vital reminder of the essential dignity of a truly professional relationship.

So then, and in conclusion, what would I like you to take from this paper?

No doubt partly because I am in old age, I would like social workers to give a bit more time to history. I am thinking of two kinds of history here. First, although in direct work with children the focus is on the 'here and now', it must be informed by a sense of the importance of the child's history in relation to the behaviour of the present. This seems dreadfully obvious but, as early as the 1990s, commentators such as David Howe were noting that we seemed to be neglecting the vital significance of the past in relation to the present. This is of course, not simply about facts but the feelings it has generated in the children. I am haunted by the episode recounted to me about a social worker who turned up at a Review Case Conference for an immigrant young person without 'reading the file' and did not know that the child's parents had been murdered. She asked him whether he wanted to go and live with his parents.

Then there is our history, our occupational and professional identity as social workers. How did we get here? What has been gained or lost in the process? It sometimes seems to me that we are caught up in a dreadful whirl of happenings, crises and instant communication; this includes, but goes far beyond, our own share of child care alarms and excursions. There is loss of collective wisdom, of a sense of continuity which gives us a framework to understand current behaviour.

Although there is a huge amount to be done to challenge the negative reporting of much in the media and the negative statements of politicians who so often have competing agendas, there is also a need to reformulate the purposes of the work and the means of achieving it. It is irresponsible not to look back and ask – how did we get here, what has been learned and what has been lost?

I have a sense that we may be on the cusp of significant change, though paradoxically at a time of particular economic difficulty and, in all probability, political change. I have seen a succession of inquiries from Maria Colwell in 1973 onwards, resulting in over-optimistic political statements about 'never again'. We have been forced to face failure in the care system, such as the poor educational attainment of children in care. There has also been far too little celebration of genuine achievements, notably in the development of fostering and adoption practice (Schofield & Simmonds, 2009). But despite this, I do hear a different voice in the discourse, in the better media, in the journals, even from the politicians on a good day, which seems to be saying that we must find better ways of using social workers to help children and their families and of supporting them to do so.

If I am right, then there is a fascinating, difficult and immensely worthwhile task awaiting us: to articulate for the early 21st century, the role of social workers in working with children who cannot live with their families or who are at risk within them. In one way, we have the advantage over the early social workers. We now have a substantial body of good research which has told us a great deal about the factors which affect the lives of children in care and the social work response to them. Our problem is not so much lack of knowledge; it is our failure to translate it into effective action.

Clare did not have the benefit of that research but she had the ability to use certain insights from psychoanalytic theory which were and are of fundamental importance to this work and which deserve our respect. As I said before, she never exaggerated the part which social workers had to play. She knew well that those who cared for children hour by hour were critical, and that it was the management of the total environment which in the end was going to make the difference between good and bad outcomes. So this is not an omnipotent claim by social workers of the centre ground. But we can use today her summing up of the three areas of work in which social workers have a particular significance.

First we try to reach the children, to establish communication and to construct a working relationship which is personal and yet structured.

Then, we try to look at his world with him and to help him sort out his feelings about it: to face the painful things and to discover the good things.

Then, we try to consolidate the positive things with the child himself and his world and help him make the most of his life.

Clare added, 'Even if we are unable to help children as much as we would like to do, we can at least attempt to prevent muddle ... or try to sort it out for them so that things add up and make some sort of sense. In this way we can prevent or relieve a great deal of distress' (1963 in Kanter 2004, p.183).

'If there is no vision, the people perish' (Proverbs: 18). In Clare's case, the vision was founded on a powerful moral view of social responsibility to the deprived or disadvantaged and of the child as a whole person, with fundamental and interacting needs – material, physical and emotional. Her vision was that social workers could play an important part in helping to meet these needs. What better for social workers today than to take that vision forward and to work out its implications for contemporary society?

References

Page references to Clare Winnicott's published work, cited here, are taken from the biography by Joel Kanter.

Bowlby J. (1997) *Attachment & Loss*, Volume 1, (revised edition), Pimlico: London

Ferguson H. (2009) 'Performing child protection: home visiting, movement and the struggle to reach the abused child', *Child & Family Social Work*, 14 (4) pp.471–80.

Kanter J. (2004) *Face to Face with Children. The Life and Work of Clare Winnicott*, Karnac Books: London.

Robertson J. & Robertson J. (1952) 'A Two-Year-Old Goes to Hospital', Concorde Film Council: Ipswich.

Schofield G. & Simmonds J. (2009) *The Child Placement Handbook: Research, policy and practice*. BAAF: London.

Vann J. (1971) 'The Child as a Client of the Social Services Department: Some Implications for the Training of Social Workers', *British Journal of Social Work*, 1 (2) pp.209–24.

Winnicott C. (1945) 'Children who cannot play', in Kanter J. (ed.) 2004, *Face to face with Children: The Life and Work of Clare Winnicott*, Karnac Books: London.

Winnicott C. (1955) 'Casework techniques in the child care services' in Kanter J. (ed.) 2004, *Face to face with Children: The Life and Work of Clare Winnicott*, Karnac Books: London.

Winnicott C. (1963) 'Face to Face with Children', in King J. (ed.) *New Thinking for Changing Needs*, Association for Social Workers: London.

Winnicott C. (1964) 'Communicating with children', *Child Care Quarterly Review*, 18(3) pp.85–93.

Winnicott, D. (1953) 'Transitional objects and transitional phenomena – A Study of the First Not-Me Possession', *International Journal of Psych-Analysis*, 34, pp.89–97.

Growing Older: What Is It Like?
Personal and Professional Reflections

I was very pleased to have been asked to give this memorial lecture since I have a high regard for the work of Counsel and Care and am glad to honour its founders. The challenge was attractive; to link the personal and the professional in a way which was not *too* self-indulgent; yet which shed light on the important ways in which personal experiences affect one's professional life and vice versa. All of us in paid work bring personal attitudes, feelings and experiences to it. It is of great importance to some of us, we react to it with particular intensity. This varies, of course, between individuals but for me work has been central to my sense of well being and fulfilment.

The process of growing older is unique to each individual. I make this point strongly because ageism, like all the 'isms', thrives on generalisations and stereotypes about 'what old people want/need/feel' etc. I make no claim to speak for others but if some things ring bells for others, so much the better. I shall try to be frank about

---

The Graham Lecture was established in 1990 to honour the founders of Counsel and Care, a charity giving advice and information to older people, their relatives and carers (now merged with Independent Age). Olive was invited to give the Lecture in 1999.

the forces and influences, positive and negative, throughout my life, which have shaped a career spanning nearly fifty years. I start from the point that growing older (from the day we are born) is part of a developmental process which does not end until we are dead, unless gross morbidity freezes the process – a tragedy we all fear. Too often, younger people deny or ignore the fact that development is a lifelong process, especially in relation to emotions and feelings, which remain powerful and significant, even when bodies deteriorate.

Just as this lecture, like music or plays, must have a shape to be enjoyed intellectually and emotionally, so must a life. To answer the question, 'What is it like to grow old?' it must be contextualised; it becomes something like 'What is it like for me, a single white woman, first-generation university educated, with a comfortable income and some status, academic and professional to be *rather* old (not *very* old by European standards) and about to enter the next millennium?'

Inevitably, in such an endeavour, one begins to search for meanings; of connections between past events and present behaviour; yet, as I pondered and fidgeted in my head, I realised that there was a danger of pretentiousness in my search for meaning. So I was much helped when I heard on Radio 4 recently that the first white sliced loaf in Britain was sold in 1930, the year of my birth. It was a reminder of the danger of false causal connections for I cannot say the loaf influenced my development profoundly, except perhaps for a strong preference for very brown unsliced bread.

There are five themes in this discussion. They are:

- The early formative years;
- Women in society and family values;
- Politics;
- Moral absolutes and moral dilemmas;
- Becoming very old.

Early Formative Years

The importance of childhood in laying the foundation for future interests and activities is self-evident. Childhood does not determine the future adult but it profoundly effects the way we see the world and our part in it. For me, it marks the beginning of my intense interest in people and their problems and of my basic values and moral framework.

I was born and brought up in the Croydon suburbs, the younger child of Irish Protestant parents. My father was an executive grade civil servant who left Dublin in 1920 when the Irish Free State was created. He feared religious discrimination at work if he stayed but then experienced racism in England. (How he hated being called 'Paddy'.) My parents brought with them to England his daughter Marjorie, aged 9, by his first marriage. His first wife had died of TB. My brother was born in 1923, that is, seven years before me.

My father was the eldest of twelve children. He had a powerful, dominant mother who managed capably on very little money. Her tiny husband, I discovered only a few years ago, worked as a public baths attendant, a secret well kept by my class-conscious relatives. My father was the one who ran to get the midwife when the next baby came. My paternal grandfather was reported to do nothing much at home except rock the cradle of the latest baby (or twins) singing 'Abide with Me'. My father's early struggles to pass examinations and support a young sick wife left their mark. He was an anxious, over-responsible man.

My mother was the second of four girls; her father was a solicitor's clerk whose early years had been almost laughably (or tragically) a stereotypically Irish male of the period; a heavy social drinker and a compulsive gambler. My grandmother was 'married off' at seventeen, very able ('a cut above buttermilk'), desperately unhappy and resentful to be trapped in poverty. (Strangely, and never explained, my maternal grandfather reformed and lived a blameless life from about fifty.) Some of the tales in my childhood revolved around his formidable mother, my maternal great-grandmother, a farmer's wife, who hid her golden sovereigns from the Sinn Fein in jars of dripping. They roamed the countryside in the years during and after the First World War, looking for funds. In his old age, he lived in Greystones, County Wicklow, a Protestant enclave where he listened only to the BBC, did the *Irish Times* crossword with a tiny stub of pencil extracted with difficulty from his waistcoat pocket and would have liked to fly the Union Jack at the bottom of the garden.

My maternal grandmother, at great personal cost, found private schools for her four daughters, ensured they all learned music (two were very talented singers) and some French. Great was the rejoicing when my mother was the first woman to be employed at the Bank of Ireland. Great was my mother's disappointment when the men at the Bank would only let her count dirty bank notes.

So we have the earliest formative influences; the 'Irishness' (whatever it means) was and still is very important to me; related to this is the sense of being alien in the suburbs ('going home' always meant to Ireland); a powerful ethos of effort and hard work (the only rebel for a time my maternal grandfather); fear of poverty and the classic snobbery of the nearly poor; distrust of Catholicism but constant efforts by my parents to avoid prejudice; Very Serious Parents who worried a lot but whose lives were lit up by shafts of wit (my father) and fits of giggles (my mother with her sisters). All the women in the family, as a psychiatrist pointed out to me many years later, where 'very powerful women' and stories about their childhood and close on-going links were central to my childhood.

Life did not allow my parents to relax for long when they came to England. They were happy to see my half-sister thrive but at seventeen years, she in turn contracted TB and died in 1935 when I was five. (Just before drug treatment became widespread.) The first five years of my life were, for my parents, years of unremitting anxiety about her, about my brother and, hugely, about me as a vulnerable infant in the house with her. Medical expenses, before the NHS, loomed large. And then in 1939, the War. My brother joined the Fleet Air Arm and in 1940 saw service mainly in the Far East (Japanese suicide bombers, etc.) and the shadow of my parents' fear hung over the household, symbolised, I recall, by the sight of a telegram boy pushing his bike up our hill. My brother came back unscathed physically, but not emotionally.

So what have those early years left with me, a very observant little girl, intensely involved with the family, watching adult pain from the sidelines? Trying to capture those times, with the episodic memories characteristic of early childhood, they are suffused with anxiety and confusion of Things Unmentionable. All families have secrets but I suspect that in those times, the 1930s, we were living in an era when 'it was better for the children not to know', perhaps a revulsion against Victorian drama about death. For the best of intentions, my parents protected me (as they thought) from their worries and fears for Marjorie. When she died, they did not tell me and I did not go to the funeral. I am left with one powerful recollection of Christmas Day 1935, in my aunt's sitting room playing bagatelle, when my father came in, flung his gloves on the table and said 'It's all over'. *What* was all over? One could not ask, I negotiated this question over the days which followed.

To my mother I said:

'Where is Marjorie?'

'She has passed away.'

But what does 'pass away' mean?

Down to the garden to my father.

'What does "passed away" mean?'

'It means died.'

'Oh.'

There was much more about which I could not ask, not least any details of my father's first marriage and of my maternal grandfather's naughty ways. (This last did not become clear to me in my parents' lifetime.) There was much shame about relatives who fell below the line of respectability; in this, as well as sad things, communications closed down.

So in this puzzled, sensitive and questioning child there developed a powerful need to understand and, I suspect, a longing to make my parents happier. And perhaps myself too. A clear recipe for social work? Certainly I sought work as a school leaver in a children's home and afterwards as an undergraduate, in vacations, with seriously emotionally disturbed children. Later, I found work in research with under-fives some of the most exciting in my professional career.

It is rather embarrassing that in many ways I had what the men sometimes called 'a good war'. I enjoyed following men round Croydon airport whom I thought might be spies; some of you may recall there was also the possibility of seeing Nazi soldiers' boots sticking out from under Nuns' clothing. I enjoyed the glamour of my officer brother's war-time leave. Tinned peaches and silk stockings from the USA. I enjoyed Blitz nights under the stairs sleeping in a deckchair, emerging at dawn to cocoa made with sweetened, condensed milk (oh, bliss!). I guess it was a welcome diversion from a family life which felt dark.

It is perhaps not surprising that when I arrived (a year late) at my grammar school at the age of twelve, I told my head teacher that I wanted to 'do' psychology when I left school. Alarmed, the head teacher wrote to my mother and said she would not recommend that I read Freud. (Which drove me to him immediately.) The die was cast for a career which, though not in psychology in the formal sense, would be dominated by an interest in the complexities and subtleties of behaviour, individual, familial, cultural and organisational.

This intense interest was further reinforced by the decision of my aunt and uncle to adopt two baby girls when I was beginning my teens. My mother and I became deeply engrossed with these two little girls and the dynamics of adoption; and differences between the children and their reactions remains with me to this day. In particular, the separation anxiety and grief which one of my cousins showed as a newly placed baby made an indelible impression on me. Then, when I was a social worker, my brother and sister-in-law also adopted two girls. The four children's dramatically different responses to adoption has powerfully affected my views on it, as has, in this year 1999, the search of one cousin and one niece for their birth families.

However, before this interest in people became formalised and professionalised, I chose to read English literature, not psychology, at University; this was a decision which I never regretted.

Words I love (the Irish in me?) and people in fact or fiction are endlessly fascinating. And the pain inherent in life is made bearable, even at times enjoyable, by the cognitive activity of making sense of it. I said goodbye (forever) to the alien suburbs and gorged on words and music at Oxford University – but flung myself into work with children in long vacations.

The real professional work began as a post-graduate student at the LSE. The die was cast for child-care social work. It would be hard to overestimate the influence of Donald and Clare Winnicott on my professional development. Donald, world famous paediatrician and psychoanalyst, Clare a psychiatric social worker (and later analyst) who was my tutor. Donald's intense interest in very young children chimed with so much which had absorbed me. It was a time when John Bowlby's work on the concept of attachment and bonding of mother to child was beginning to have a major impact on social workers in the UK (Bowlby, 1951). The adverse effects of broken attachment and of depersonalised institutional care, especially in large residential nurseries fitted my interests like a glove. It has stayed with me for ever and has been continuously reinforced by each new revelation all over the world of childhood deprivation. Early films of 'Laura' and 'John', Laura going to hospital and John to a nursery, without their mothers, are as vivid to me today as in 1952 (Robertson & Robertson, 1952). There was nothing in my own childhood to mirror that. On the contrary, I was a cherished child. But the aloneness and the bewilderment of deprived children strikes a deep chord and some of this resonates with my own childhood.

The Position of Women in Society: Family Values

Feminist theory came late to me; that is, the analysis of women's position in society which shows how the exercise of male power has been oppressive to women. I was slow in identifying with that body of theory which hit us in the 1960s and 1970s. Indeed, the first real sense I had that feminism had come of age was at a summer Social Policy Association Conference sometime in the early 1970s. I was alerted to it by the visible outbreak of body hair, legs and armpits, which surrounded me whilst I, older and old-fashioned, persisted with a razor.

It seems strange now that I had got left behind. After all, there were forces in my background which led me to respect and admire my forceful women relatives. I was fascinated early on when I realised that my aunt, a professional singer, used her 'maiden' name in that role.

In Purley, where I lived as a child, I knew ten or twelve single women. They intrigued me enormously, the more so when it was explained to me that some had lost their fiancés in the 1914–1918 War. How many, I know not. No doubt it was a face-saving device for some at a time when marriage was a woman's goal. But for reasons I have never quite understood, since it was not 'my war', that war, the waste and the grief of it, made a huge impression on me and I watched these women with a kind of awed sympathy. To this day, I shed tears on Armistice Day, yet none of my relatives died in that war. (My father was in the British Army, however. I wore his army cap when I rode my tricycle.) I noted that most of these women were friendly and busy, at least outwardly cheerful. They had adjusted to single life and restricted income with dignity and competence. They had 'little jobs', as they were described – in Boots Lending Library for instance. This made me uncomfortable.

As I became middle-aged, I grew much more aware of my privileged childhood. First, and perhaps foremost, my father and equally my mother, never for one moment implied that education was less important for me than my brother and they gave me their unremitting support for five years of higher education at considerable financial cost. (My father retired the year I went to University.) My brother too helped support me financially at University. Secondly, I was always encouraged (and not reluctant!) to express opinions and to argue. Thirdly, my academic success and articulacy singled me out, especially when I entered social work. There I was a big fish in a small pond. Despite terrible miseries at school and emotional torment in early years at university, my intellectual confidence was high in the early period of my career. I entered social work in child care at a time when, for reasons not wholly admirable or logical, but beneficial to many women, social work was regarded as 'women's work' and there were no barriers to my progress.

In academia, as a single and childless woman, I experienced little or no prejudice and was one of few women professors in the 1970s. The prejudice was directed towards social work. My career was not held back by family commitments. I entered the world of the Social Sciences and was cushioned from the male bias of academics in other disciplines, such as medicine and science. Looking back, I was remarkably insensitive to the position of many women.

Nonetheless, I was fighting some internal battles, of which I was only partly aware. My mother never worked and set a model of 'domestic caring' which I have internalised, without often needing to use it. My mother always being at home, with the bacon grilling when I came in hungry from school, was taken for granted in my young life. I was, as people have said, spoilt, all things being geared to my study needs.

But this nurturing has left an indelible mark on me; as a woman, I have expected to do the same, for example, for friends and relatives, for whom there must be a meal ready and waiting when they come in. The nice bit about this is that it is experienced as warm and welcoming and gives pleasure to both sides. But what on earth would I have been like if there had been ordinary family demands on me? Certainly, spells looking after an elderly aunt in recent years have left vivid memories of internal tensions between 'getting on with my writing work' and needing to be with her, who wanted company. What I am suggesting is that, as a girl, one may internalise values and expectations of how is it to be a woman at home, which are often based on an experience of a mother who was respected and loved for what she was. (Processes of identification are complex.) Perhaps it is significant that, in the last few years, when I have been less frantic about work (everything is relative!), I have enjoyed more than ever before aspects of domestic activity, notably cooking, yes, and shopping, which were the centre of my mother's world. (Not *exactly*: I do not worry about Swiss Rolls splitting when they come out of the oven. But I still cut carrots the same way.) I think it is interesting that although I have not experienced the divided loyalties which so many women experience, I nonetheless have been aware of feeling ill at ease when either side of my life – domestic or professional – swamps the other.

There is however, another aspect to this theme and my internal struggles about which I would feel dishonest if I did not comment. From my early adolescence, I became aware that my sexual identity was probably lesbian (though the word was unknown, except in dreadfully secret and rude literature). Mention of the island Lesbos was enough to send a shiver down the spine and the novel *The Well of Loneliness* was kept well away from family eyes. The consequences of that discovery are too complex to discuss here. But in the years of which I am speaking, it was an issue about which family conversation was impossible; an area of huge importance was walled off, sadly, and not unblocked in my parents' lifetime, just as my half-sister's death had been blocked off all those years ago. Thus, the expectation of my family that I would be married was painful. My teens and early twenties were full of deceit and denial; at Oxford, the realisation that there were others like me helped a lot, but I was still left with a powerful sense of conflict between feelings that this was right for me and doubts and fears about stigma, about being 'deviant'. I sought help over a period of four years between 1950 and 1954 from three doctors; one, a GP, told me that I was the wrong shape to be a lesbian; the second, a psychiatrist, told me that my powerful women ancestors made it impossible to change; the third, a psychologist, told me it was OK but that such relationships were, of course, sterile.

He was right in a sense, but the word 'sterile' was like a dagger. I have felt the need on occasion for younger people to know about such experiences the better to understand the changes I and others have had to confront over these fifty years.

Of course, at that time, children were ruled out for me. So much so that I was not aware of wanting my own children, although keenly interested in other people's. Indeed, my first writing professionally was rooted in the observations of young children, first, as a post-graduate student, about the 'transitional objects', or 'cuddlies' which little children may find essential and, in my first academic post, a book for foster parents of young children. It would not be true to say that these interests emerged because I was a childless lesbian. As you have seen, they were rooted far earlier than that. What this does illustrate, however, is the capacity which we have to sublimate normal drives – such as having children – into rewarding and enriching activities which may benefit others but are also deeply satisfying of one's own needs.

For me, the door was simply closed. I did not think (and did not fret about it) to have or bring up children. In my lifetime, the behaviour and assumptions about family structures have radically changed. I have not found it easy to move with the times but have now reached the point at which most of my early doubts about the creation of lesbian families seem to have been ill-founded. Indeed research does not support them. In a sense it is a benign circle. For, as society's prejudice against lesbian relationships diminishes, their children are less likely to experience the pain and stigma which I feared.

More generally, however, I remain rather intolerant about the attitudes of women (whatever their sexual preference) who seem to regard having a child as a right and a necessity for their mental health. Such insight as I have does not tell me that this is simply my sour reaction. But I do recognise and regret that I have not always been understanding enough to those younger women whose needs are felt more urgently, because revolutions in social attitudes and fertility treatment make possible that which was impossible even to contemplate in my earlier years. I repent of this.

Two final personal postscripts on children. It is paradoxical that I have felt more envious in very recent years of other peoples' grandchildren. This links consciously with a fear of being personally out of touch with the young generation, but I suspect it is deeper than that. It would be nice to have the fun without the role conflict of earlier years.

Politics

If you have noted my word portrait of my parents, you may have guessed that they read the *Daily Telegraph*. My father was, by conviction, a Conservative, who revered Winston Churchill, and whose patriotism was tinged with the desperation of being part of a Protestant minority in Ireland and who needed law and order, the hallmark of conservatism, to control his many painful anxieties. My mother could easily have been detached from the Right of politics. Her natural affinities were liberal. She enjoyed the *Telegraph* only for its excellent reporting of scandal and went to her afternoon rest to enjoy such tales as the dinner parties of the Duchess of Argyll, who entertained her guests in the nude. (The servants wore aprons.) My brother who became a very successful businessman, muttered through clenched teeth in his later years, apropos apparently of nothing, 'Don't knock the multi-nationals' (I didn't know what he meant at the time).

At some point, coinciding roughly with the end of the War and the election of the Labour government, I became aware that there were alternative political scenarios. I cannot describe the shock in the family when Winston Churchill fell from power after the War. We were staggered. It felt so disloyal. But, somewhere, Radical Thoughts were ticking over in my mind and the family never ceased to remind me of the time (I was 19 or 20) when I screamed at my sister-in-law, 'You are like Marie-Antoinette – you say, let them eat cake!'

Of course, my teens were in the formative post-war years of the welfare state. I noticed political propaganda for the first time. The logic of socialism was to me persuasive and its social goals much more compatible with the daily kind and humane behaviour of those I loved than some of their words, which reflected more their fear of revolution, change and disorder (Reds looked for under the beds), than oppressive, repressive or illiberal attitudes to other people. The men, father and a favourite uncle and brother, were very *benign* Tories, whose position in society had been hard won and who believed that others could make the effort and be upwardly mobile as they had been.

We jogged along quite comfortably in the new welfare state, taking full advantage of health and education services. I leaned to the left but in the early years of my career flung myself into social work without a sharp sense of party political identity or a need to involve myself in that struggle.

And then, after more than twenty years of this personal accommodation to politics came the Thatcher regime. I was uneasy, for we had had warning signs before the election of a deep antagonism to 'welfare'. In 1980, when I gave the Eleanor Rathbone Memorial lecture, I concluded:

> The British tradition of gradualism works both ways. We reform slowly; do we also de-reform slowly? Are we witnessing shifts in emphasis, for example, as between the voluntary and statutory sectors, which in the long run may be seen to be beneficial, or are we seeing the very foundations of community care in a developed society being gradually undermined? It is not to be expected that an Act for the dissolution of the welfare state will be promulgated. Yet there are actions, including the enactment of laws and gnomic statements, which in aggregate at least point to the need for keen vigilance.
>
> …
>
> But for us in Britain in the 1980s, given the subtleties of our political processes, vigilance must be the watchword. It is no good tending the trees if there has been planning permission to cut the forest down.
>
> (Stevenson, 1980, p.29)

That feels quite prophetic.

The eighteen years of the Conservative administration were not, in my view, entirely negative – that would be nonsense. But for me they were, in every imaginable way, most traumatic. At a personal level, they challenged my assumptions about social values and about the structures by which social values are transmitted. At a professional level, these years saw the beginning of a political attack on social work, which had been the pivot of my working life. More selfishly, I resented my exclusion from the world of government. For example, for four years before the election at the end of the

1970s, I had been a Member of the Royal Commission on Compensation for Personal Injury and had enjoyed the feeling of involvement in that world – not only for status and its trappings – but also for the intellectual challenge and a chance to change a few things. In 1980, I slid unnoticed on to the Social Security Advisory Committee, where I still sit, but for the next seventeen years of the Tory administration I was in a politico-social wilderness. No more grand government committees for me. After all, there was no such thing as society and social work was naff.

Much, much worse were the sinking feelings as certain cherished values and institutions were undermined. Although I worried about policy changes which reflected values I did not agree with, I worried as much, as time went on, about what I can only term *state negligence*, driven by reflections, indifference, ignorance and political dogma. Two examples out of many are: first, the refusal by the previous administration to regulate the rising tide of private independent domiciliary agencies struck me as scandalous. I had come to accept the need for a better balance of provision between state and independent sectors – and not just for financial reasons. But at a time when the numbers of very old people were increasing and, within them, a substantial number vulnerable to abuse and exploitation, it seemed inexcusable not to put in safeguards.

The second issue over which my blood pressure soared was the withdrawal of benefit to 16 and 17 year-olds living away from home unless they could prove good reason for being away. (Even that concession was hard won.) Years of benefit watching and advising has convinced me that the Social Security system is incapable of addressing with sufficient subtlety the unique human situations which arise and in awarding some benefits. The abused step-child may be too shamed or frightened and fearful for their brothers and sisters to tell her story of running away; the slick ones, who know how to work the system, may tell it all too well. Even more fundamental was the failure to look sensibly at the evidence: the likelihood of well-cared-for 16 and 17 year-olds leaving and *staying away* from home for the so-called bright lights was remote. Since this paragraph was first drafted, evidence has revealed how many were young people fresh from 'care of the local authorities' (another dreadful story), or abusive homes.

What a way to conduct social policy. How narrow and perverse. Concern about this crossed party politics. One notes the brave stand on this taken by the late Baroness Faithfull, a Tory peer, who really knew about child welfare.

These comments, incidentally, reflect another long-standing interest. In 1968, I was seconded from the University of Oxford for two years to be Social Work Advisor to the (then) Supplementary Benefits Commission. I became very interested in what the social security was good at and what it was bad at. That and subsequent experience has shown me that whilst an efficient social security system can and should deliver universal benefits fairly and reliably, it rarely succeeds when the needs are highly individualised, bound up with the particular circumstances of individuals. I analysed and argued this in 1970, in the book which marked that chapter in my life (Stevenson, 1970).

So those eighteen years, lasting until I retired from the University were sad in many ways. It meant that I had to accept the work in which I had invested so heavily for nearly forty years, whilst not worthless, was not valued (or so it felt) as I would have hoped. (I don't deny an element of vanity and competitiveness.) It meant that my very naïve assumptions about social 'progress', a view of history I should have shed years before, were overturned. My psychological security, which kept depression at bay, had been based on a belief that effort could make things better. This is true, of course, but, a lot of the time, professional life is about not letting things get worse. Perhaps the best one can do is follow Blake and accept that 'he who could do good must do it in minute particulars'! These thoughts may reflect a modest achievement of my growing older – to be less omnipotent.

Looking back, I also note that the liberty my parents gave me to express and develop my views was paradoxically a foundation for the formation of my own political values which differed from theirs, at least from my father's. Further, the example they showed me in their daily lives, notably of courtesy and tenderness to people outside the immediate family, gave me the basis for these values which emphasised fraternity (and sorority) and equality as well as liberty. They contributed to a conviction of the need for political balance, for movement on the political continuum.

Thus are we moulded but not determined!

Moral Absolutes & Moral Dilemmas

Moral absolutes can be reassuring, apparently giving a framework for certainties. For me, they were fuelled by anger and outrage as I became aware of the world outside. I was protected from many horrors of wartime but seeing the first post-war films of the concentration camps enabled me to make connections with the loving care my Aunt and Uncle had shown to two Jewish refugees from Austria and Germany who lived with their family. Mimi, officially a domestic help, lightened our lives with wit and cookery demonstrations (of paper thin pastry for strudel and delicious cabbage soup) and was still in touch at the end of my Aunt's life. Herman, a schoolboy who eventually went to the USA with his parents sought her out when he was in his fifties. These and others I have loved in later life are the real Jewish people who give meaning to the Holocaust and I weep for those I did not know. Then, in Oxford, I heard Trevor Huddleston and saw his eyes blazing with anger. The horror of South African apartheid became real. Much later, I taught a black woman student from Soweto and learned of the struggle for education, for example, of damaged eyesight from reading without electricity, of the endless need to be grateful to those who provided opportunities; layer upon layer, my awareness of men's and women's inhumanity to each other deepened and reinforced personal and professional values.

However, the comfort of moral absolution is not enough. For me, there are two problems. The first are imaginative limitations. Looking back, I can see I was slow to appreciate the significance of racial oppression in our own country. And this is not only about racism. It is as true of the other 'isms' – of my insensitivity to issues, concerning disabled people for example. It is perhaps something about taking for granted what is around day-by-day; too close to see?

To be fair, I suppose all of us are children of our times, with a view of our society which is partial and unreflective until we are jolted into awareness. But I have private moments of shame about my slow realisation of flagrant injustices, under my nose. I plead 'not guilty', however, to minimising ageism in society, at least from the 1970s onwards. I needed for my own good the mini-revolution in social work education in the 1980s when all the 'isms' but especially racism, dominated the discourse of anti-oppressive practice. But it also led me to identify more clearly a second problem which I have with moral absolutes. In daily life, we have to make choices between lesser evils and also between opposing goods. In child welfare, an example of 'lesser evils' which became a 'hot potato' concerned foster or adoptive placements for black or mixed-heritage children. As we became more aware of the huge importance of 'identity' formation, I realised this had to be balanced against the equally important concept of attachment. And we ran into dreadful difficult decisions about placing with, or moving mixed-heritage children from, white foster parents. The debates polarised, with much harsh and inaccurate criticism of social workers but also some wrong-headed decisions taken by them (or by inflexible left-wing local authorities). Teaching at that time was for me, deeply uncomfortable. As I have said elsewhere '... there was a whiff of McCarthyism in the air' (Stevenson, 1998). An example of 'opposing goods' comes from China where I went annually for five years to develop social work education. Their primary focus was on services for old people. Their concerns arose from the effects of the ruthless 'one child policy', which changed the demographic balance so greatly that there were no longer sufficient children to care, when adults, for their old people in the family. And yet China has controlled their population where India has failed and this is hugely important to their progress – including the position of women.

I get very cross about the moral certainties of some Human Rights workers who find it particularly convenient to detect abuses a long way from their own country.

In fact, this tendency to think in terms of 'on the one hand' and 'on the other' has been a difficulty in my professional life. It has made me feel at times isolated, when I could not join wholeheartedly in a particular crusade. This is sometimes a failure of nerve but it is also a real distrust of fanaticism which often accompanies crusades. The biographer of Isaiah Berlin reports that he shared with Alfred Brendel, the pianist, 'fixed dislikes of noise, cigarette smoke and fanaticism' (Ignatieff, 1998). That feels right to me.

This rather gloomy analysis of the Thatcher years and of social work education is not, however, the whole story of that period. For my working life has never been devoid of challenge. As my 'government niche' disappeared, opportunities arose to become more directly involved with issues concerning ageing. What I have told you of earlier years has focused on child welfare but this is in fact only part of the story. Picking another part of my life story, in the 1980s, I made a considered decision to develop research and teaching interests in ageing, in particular in the needs of vulnerable and frail very old people. The demographic trends suggested that this issue was going to be vitally important in social policy and social care. However, I am doubtful that my reasons were purely intellectual and rational. Quite what they were, I am not sure. My parents did not live to old age or require care and the elderly aunt from whom I was to learn so much about vulnerability in very old age was not at that time needing care. Nor was I at a stage when my own ageing loomed large. However, I can trace a theme. Long ago, as a student with the Family Welfare Association I had grieved over 'Percy', an old man living in a basement in Paddington. He was utterly alone; I, young and foolish, promised to keep in touch with him and did not do so. Again, this theme of loneliness and isolation emerges. It remains for me a particularly poignant aspect of the lives of some very old people that they are emotionally or physically alone in their last years.

From a professional point of view, an opportunity arose to consolidate and widen my interests when in the early 1980s I was invited to become Chair of Age Concern England. This most effectively distracted me from sulking about Mrs Thatcher. I learned so much, not only about age but about the workings of the voluntary sector. A whole new world opened up to me, which has never closed down. The significance of those years was epitomised by my choice of topic 'Women in Old Age' for my inaugural lecture at Nottingham University in 1986. As we moved into the 1990s, my aunt's deteriorating mental condition, and the painful challenge of finding her appropriate residential care in the last years, was one of the steepest of my learning curves. It stimulated quite deep thought about the challenge to personal autonomy which developing mental incapacity brings, and the dilemmas for relatives. And it enabled me to pursue one of my favourite intellectual activities, making connections and links. I began to join up thoughts on child protection with the protection of very old people from abuse. It also forced me to confront the doubts which I had long held about that part of anti-ageism rhetoric which seemed to deny the reality of failing bodies and minds in a substantial number of very old people. You know what I mean – the often cited examples of unusual people of 103 who go parachuting or write encyclopaedias.

So there is a consistency in my link across the generations; it has a strong protective urge in it, which I well realise has dangers as well as strengths.

Very Old Age

To claim very old age these days, before one is seventy, or indeed, eighty or ninety, is absurd. But I am aware, as many people here will be, that if many more years lie ahead, there are serious challenges. I cannot claim to have experienced the 'little old lady' oppression which is still so prevalent in today's society and I rarely get patronised. (Perhaps that is why the AA man's question, on seeing my rather smart coupé, 'Can you handle the power?' still rankles.) I am too formidable for this and *may* be destined for the 'Isn't she wonderful?' category if I am not careful. But this kind of comment is inherently ageist; it usually means doing the *unusual*. It demeans the millions of elderly men and women (but more women at the moment) who *are* wonderful because they survive and adapt magnificently to the ordinary unseen sadness of loss, poverty and disability and of managing life alone. I am trying to learn from their examples. I don't think I will be poor (though you never know); if I live, I will have to experience the loss of my contemporaries including very dear friends. But I am accustomed to the role of a coping woman on her own; indeed, the problem for me (anyone else here?) will be managing decently the transition to greater dependence, certainly physical and possibly intellectual (a dread). Both of which could involve greater emotional dependence than I would welcome.

An aspect of very old age which nags at me constantly is my technological inadequacy. I will spare you the boring details but I (surely not alone?) have become increasingly aware that both professionally and personally my failure to master computers so far is serious. Professionally, I am embarrassed: 'What a pity you are not on email'; personally, it seems to me a necessity to do so for my old age. Shopping 'online', for example, offers huge possibilities to reduce dependence on others. We will all have our personal explanations or excuses. But I am interested to observe in myself the undercurrent of worry it causes and the fear of social exclusion it raises. Anyone else?

The third of the issues (poverty and loss being the other two) to be faced is ill health. I think for my generation there are big problems in this. Most people are reasonably fit and active until their last years. But there are 'imitations' of mortality long before that, not in the sense of imminent death but in a raised awareness of health issues, of having to pay attention to our bodies and, in my case, resenting the time and anxiety such problems cause. More fundamentally, perhaps, is the awareness in a body-conscious age, of declining physical attractiveness and (let's face it) of deterioration. I think that this may be particularly strong in women. Or are men's fears better hidden? Then, in the last years there is the problem of what is gloomily called 'compressed morbidity', as a result of a traumatic episode or degenerative condition. To find ways of preventing these diseases or successfully rehabilitating sufferers is a huge challenge to research and to medicine. Without such advances, there will be many who question the whole notion of 'successful ageing' and greatly increased life expectancy.

Meanwhile, we have to make practical and emotional plans for very old age each within our own personal context. For me, there is no virtue in the 'it may never happen' approach (which is not the same as over-anxious preoccupation). Our society has singularly failed to raise sensible awareness at an early stage of the things we need to reflect on and plan for in that phase. These, of course, range across the whole spectrum of human need. As you have gathered, changed levels of dependency is an issue for me – and I guess it is for many others. I would also very much like not to be a bore over trivialities with friends and relations, as I stay in more and wait in vain for plumbers or electricians. I would like my listening and not my whinging capacity to increase. Some of you will know of the debate amongst psychologists about the concept of 'wisdom' in the intelligence of older people. It's a *lovely*, cosy idea. The younger are quicker off the mark but, boy, are our judgements sound! I do not discount this but I suspect that for such wisdom to be perceived as valuable it must be in part derived from an understanding of the contemporary world as well as the past. Some dilemmas are eternal but how these are addressed must take account of the Now, not just past experience. That poses a challenge, not only for my generation but for society as a whole. It is an aspect of social inclusion which the present Government has barely touched. Did you notice the Government spokesman hesitate recently when questions were raised as to whether any of the cheap computers were to be made available to older people?

Now, of course, I must end with death! I do not have a religious faith; neither did my non church-going parents. I went to church as a child and young person, encouraged by a devout aunt but throughout those years did not experience any kind of religious conviction and thus it has remained. I am not atheist, simply agnostic. I cannot identify with the central tenets of the Christian faith.

Like many others, I am not afraid of death but of dying. Residual omnipotence makes me want to control arrangements to mark my passing and I spend too much rather pleasurable time thinking about the detail of a funeral event, when words and music (my two passions) can be used to good effect. Now this is, I think, an important point for my generation. Lack of religious identification makes a Christian funeral, for me, simply wrong. But the beauty and familiar comfort occurs for most of us within that tradition. I believe profoundly in the reassurance of ritual. I know that some people manage such rituals outside church with dignity and that the bereaved can really enjoy them. But I fear the funereal equivalent of the Registry office wedding and, not being an earthy sort of person, gathering around trees in the rain is not my sort of thing. (Yes, I know I won't be there.)

The point is a serious one. We all need to think about the ways in which we can respond sensitively to the wishes and needs of the hundred and thousands, perhaps millions, of people who are not committed to any religious faith. Furthermore, some with or without religious faith need to have their lifestyle and sexual orientation at life's end acknowledged by such symbols as who sits at the front of the church/hall/synagogue, who are the chief mourners. An 'event' which marks death in ways which make them seem real to those who grieve needs to be supported by our social arrangements. These are all indicators of social inclusion until the end of life for elderly people who are unique as individuals.

Conclusion

That is the end of this journey. Thank you for your patience. I conclude with a quotation from Trotsky cited by my intellectual hero, Isaiah Berlin. Trotsky was indeed a 'Red', not under, but *on* the bed. Berlin was a Liberal in the best sense of the much maligned word. A nice juxtaposition. Trotsky said: 'Anyone desiring a quiet life has done badly to be born in the twentieth century' (Ignatieff, 1998). With a bit of luck I will make it into the 21st century. I doubt if I will have a quieter life.

References

Blake W., 'Jerusalem', f.55 l.54.

Bowlby J. (1951), *Child Care and the Growth of Love*, Penguin: London.

Ignatieff M. (1998), *A Life: Isaiah Berlin*, Chatto and Windus: London.

Robertson J. & Robertson J. (1952), 'A Two-Year-Old Goes to Hospital', Concorde Film Council: Ipswich.

Stevenson O. (1970), *Claimant or Client? A Social Worker's View of the Supplementary Benefits Commission*, Allen & Unwin: London.

Stevenson O. (1980), 'The Realities of a Caring Community', Eleanor Rathbone Memorial Lecture, Liverpool University.

Stevenson O. (1986), 'Women in Old Age', Inaugural Lecture, Nottingham University.

Postscript

I first met Olive in March 2000 when she came to see me. This was the year she turned seventy and she was looking for a psychotherapist. She spoke about her various professional and academic roles, of how her early life had influenced her choices in terms of career and how she had always believed in reflective practice and had fostered its use among her colleagues. All this time I had the feeling that this impressive and articulate woman was interviewing me at least as much as I was assessing her. In the previous year, Counsel and Care had invited her to give the 1999 Graham Lecture. The subject was 'Growing Older: What is it Like?' Two features of her lecture stand out: one, her emphasis on childhood influences continuing into old age and two, the fact that all of life is a developmental process, personal as well as professional, emotional as well as intellectual.

Certainly, the issue of ageing was on her mind at that time and it is typical of Olive's thoroughness that she wanted to invest in a chance to explore again the childhood experiences which had made her what she had become and also to provide herself with an ongoing opportunity to reflect on her current life, its necessary triumphs and disasters, and its progression towards an inevitable end. Never afraid to confront orthodoxy with the difficult questions she wanted at this stage in her life to challenge herself with a careful scrutiny of her emotional and intellectual convictions and the impact these would have on decisions she made as her age increased.

Her experience of life was always visceral as well as intellectual and, when she was advised to go on a diet, we spent some time reflecting on the relationship she had developed with food as a child. First, as mentioned in these memoirs, her distressed mother might not have had enough milk to feed her and subsequently she had the experience of being a child in wartime Britain where the scarcity of food gave it the aura of the ultimate good. For the rest of her life Olive worried if she had to miss a meal. And it was as a part of her appetite for 'making sense of things' that Olive recently began writing these vivid and lively memoirs. All this reflects the vigorous and robust woman she had become; however, it is also important to remember the central message she gave me during that first encounter nearly thirteen years ago.

With her usual clarity she told me that she could feel trapped by her professional reputation for competence, management, courage, determination and so on: all the qualities I have been commenting on. Trapped within this vision that people had of her she could begin to neglect the anxious, bewildered, sometimes unhappy, occasionally lonely, potentially dependent, possibly child-like person she was as well. (How, otherwise, could she have known so much about the neglected members of society?) We needed, said Olive, to give this person some attention and we did. It was on the basis of that first interview that Olive gave me the job of accompanying her on this significant journey and for the rest of my life I will be glad and proud that she did. It has been a tremendous privilege to work with her up to and through the present time and what I have learned from her about how to live I hope never to forget.

Jane Campbell
2013

Bibliography
Published Works
by Olive Stevenson

Books

As Author

(1964) *Someone Else's Child: a Book for Foster Parents*, Routledge & Kegan Paul: Oxford (1977, 2nd edn).

(1973) *Claimant or Client? A Social Worker's View of the Supplementary Benefits Commission*, Allen & Unwin: London.

(1988) *Age and Vulnerability: a Guide to Better Care*, Edward Arnold: London.

(1998) *Neglected Children and their Families*, Blackwell Science: Oxford (2007, 2nd edn).

(1998) *Neglected Children: Issues and Dilemmas*, Blackwell Science: Oxford (2007, 2nd edn).

As Editor

(1981) *Specialisation in Social Service Teams*, Allen & Unwin: London.

(1989) *Child Abuse: Professional Practice and Public Policy*, Harvester Wheatsheaf: Harlow/London.

(1998) *Child Welfare in the UK*, Blackwell Science: Oxford.

As Co-author and Co-editor

Cooper J. D. & Stevenson O. (1980) *Social Groupwork with Elderly People in Hospital*, Beth Johnson Foundation: Stoke-on-Trent.

Hallett C. & Stevenson O. (1980) *Child Abuse: Aspects of Inter-professional Cooperation*, Allen & Unwin: London.

Stevenson O. & Fuller R. (1983) *Policies, Programmes & Disadvantage*, Heinemann: London.

———— & Lynch M. (1990) *Report on the Death of Stephanie Fox*, Wandsworth Borough Council: London.

Stevenson O. (guest ed.) (2005) *Child and Family Social Work*, 10 (3).

Stevenson O. & Charles M. (eds) (1991) *Multidisciplinary is Different: Child Protection, Working Together*; vol. 1: *The Process of Learning and Training*, Nottingham University Press: Nottingham.

———— & Charles M. (eds) (1991) *Multidisciplinary is Different: Child Protection, Working Together*; vol. 2: *Sharing Perspectives*, Nottingham University Press: Nottingham.

———— & Parsloe P. (eds) (1993) *Community Care & Empowerment*, Joseph Rowntree Foundation: York.

———— & Parsloe P. (eds) (1978) *Social Service Teams, the Practitioner's View*, HMSO: London.

Articles, Chapters & Papers

(1954), 'The First Treasured Possession: A study of the part played by specially loved objects and toys in the lives of certain children', *Psychoanalytic Study of the Child*, 9.

(1961) 'Integration of Theory and Practice in Professional Training', *Case Conference*, 8 (20) pp.45–9.

(1962) 'Maintaining the Links: our Role with Parents', *Accord* (Journal of the Association of Child Care Officers), pp.27–44.

(1963) 'Co-ordination Reviewed', *Case Conference*, 9 (8) pp.208–12.

(1963) 'Reception into Care: its Meaning for all Concerned', *Case Conference*, 10 (4) pp.110–14.

(1963) 'The Skills of Supervision: a Study of Teaching Method' (paper), *New Thinking for Changing Needs* (papers given at the Study Conference of the Association of Social Workers), pp.66–80.

(1963) 'The Understanding Caseworker', *New Society*, 1 August, pp.84–96.

(1964) 'The Challenge of Family Social Work Today' (paper), *New Barnett Papers 1: The Family in Modern Society* (papers given at the Study Conference of the Association of Social Workers), pp.48–63.

(1964) 'Intuition and Involvement in Social Work', *The Almoner*, 17 (1) pp.3–6.

(1966) 'Social Work and Training: the Next Phase', *Case Conference*, 12 (7) pp.235–39.

(1967) 'Co-ordination Reviewed', Younghusband E. (ed.), *Social Work and Social Values. Readings in Social Work*, vol. 3 pp.113–20.

(1967) 'New Thinking about Institutional Care: Summing Up' (paper), *New Thinking about Institutional Care* (papers given at the Study Conference of the Association of Social Workers), pp.76–82.

(1968) 'Specialisation within a Unified Service', *Case Conference*, 15 (5) pp.184–89.

(1969) 'The Problems of Individual Need and Fair Shares for All',
    Social Work Today, 1 (1) pp.15–21.

(1969) 'Welfare: Problems and Priorities' (paper), *New Thinking
    about Welfare: Values and Priorities* (papers given at the Study
    Conference of the Association of Social Workers) pp.76–89.

(1970) 'Care or Control: a View of Intermediate Treatment',
    Social Work Today, pp.3–6.

(1971), Editorial, *British Journal of Social Work*, 1(1) pp.1–3.

(1971) 'Knowledge for Social Work', *British Journal of Social Work*,
    1 (2) pp.225–37.

(1971) 'Relationships between Educators and Practitioners in
    Social Work' (paper), *Social Work Education in the 1970s*
    (papers given at the Study Conference of the Association of
    Social Workers), pp.103–12.

(1972) 'Strengths and Weaknesses in Residential Care', inaugural
    lecture of the Quetta Rabley Memorial, June.

(1973) 'The Exercise of Discretion', Stevenson O. (ed.), *Claimant
    or Client? A Social Worker's View of the Supplementary Benefits
    Commission*, Allen & Unwin, London, pp.38–59.

(1973) 'Stigma and Need', Stevenson O. (ed.), *Claimant or
    Client? A Social Worker's View of the Supplementary Benefits
    Commission*, Allen & Unwin, London, pp.13–37.

(1975) 'Control without Custody' (paper), the Cropwood
    Conference, December.

(1976) 'The Development of Social Work Education', Halsey A.H.
    (ed.), *Traditions of Social Policy*, Blackwell Science: Oxford,
    pp.123–44.

(1976) 'Some Dilemmas in Social Work Education', *Oxford
    Review of Education*, 2 (2) pp.149–55.

(1978) 'Ageing: a Professional Perspective', Age Concern
    (occasional papers): London.

(1978) 'Practice: an Overview. The Social Worker's Experience of
    Work', Stevenson O. & Parsloe P. (eds), *Social Service Teams,
    the Practitioner's View*, HMSO: London, pp.297–326.

(1978) 'Seebohm: Seven Years On', *New Society*, 43 (800)
    pp.249–50.

(1978) 'Some Educational Implications', Stevenson O. & Parsloe P. (eds), *Social Service Teams, the Practitioner's View*, HMSO: London, pp.329–59.

(1980) 'Social Service Teams in the United Kingdom', Lonsdale S., Webb W., & Briggs T.L. (eds), *Teamwork in the Personal Social Services and Health Care: British and American Perspectives*, Croom Helm: London, pp.9–32.

(1981) 'Caring and Dependency', Hobman D. (ed.), *The Impact of Ageing*, Croom Helm: London, pp.128–42.

(1981) 'It's Time to be All', *Community Care*, April, pp.18–20.

(1981) 'The Issues in Context', Stevenson O. (ed.), *Specialisation in Social Service Teams*, Allen & Unwin: London, pp.13–47.

(1981) 'The Notion of Expertise', Stevenson O. (ed.), *Specialisation in Social Service Teams*, Allen & Unwin: London, pp.48–59.

(1981) 'The Realities of a Caring Community', Eleanor Rathbone Memorial Lecture, Liverpool University Press: Liverpool.

(1981) 'Substitute Care: Aspects of Research and Policy', *Association of Child Psychology and Psychiatry Newsletter*, 7 pp.1–6.

(1983) 'Reflections on the Barclay Report: a Review Article', *Journal of Social Policy*, 12 (3) pp.235–45.

(1983) 'Research and Policy in the Personal Social Services', Gandy J., Robertson A. & Sinclair S. (eds), *Improving Social Intervention*, Croom Helm: London, pp.22–53.

(1985) 'The Changing Role of Social Services Departments' (paper), Association of Directors of Social Services, March.

(1985) 'Education for Community Care', *British Medical Journal*, Green College Lectures.

(1985) 'Elderly People and Visual Impairment', *The British Journal for Visual Impairment*, 3 (3) pp.71–74.

(1986) 'Guest Editorial on the Jasmine Beckford Enquiry', *British Journal of Social Work*, 16 pp.501–10.

(1986) 'The Personal Social Services', Wilding P. (ed.), *In Defence of the Welfare State*, Manchester University Press: Manchester, pp.98–126.

(1986) 'Women in Old Age: Reflections on Policy' (pamphlet), School of Social Studies, University of Nottingham: Nottingham.

(1987) 'Implications of Recent Child Care Research for the Future Organisation of Services', *Creative Social Work with Families*, British Association of Social Workers: Birmingham, pp.10–20.

(1988) 'Law and Social Work Education', *Issues in Social Work Education*, 8 (1) pp.31–7.

(1988) 'Multidisciplinary Work: Where Next?', *Child Abuse Review*, 2 (1).

(1988) 'The Next Twenty Years: Can Community Care be a Reality?' (lecture), the Diocese of Leicester Board for Social Responsibility, November.

(1988) 'Practice Issues Arising from Enquiries' (paper), conference of the British Association of Social Workers, February.

(1989) 'The Challenge of Inter-agency Collaboration', *Adoption and Fostering*, 13 (1).

(1989) 'Empowerment and Opportunity' (paper), conference of the British Association of Social Workers, April.

(1989) 'Multidisciplinary Work in Child Protection', Stevenson O. (ed.), *Child Abuse: Public Policy and Professional Practice*, Harvester Wheatsheaf: Harlow, pp.173–203.

(1989) 'Reflections on Social Work Practice', Stevenson O. (ed.), *Child Abuse: Public Policy and Professional Practice*, Harvester Wheatsheaf: Harlow, pp.145–72.

(1989) 'Taken from Home', Shardlow S. (ed.), *The Values of Change in Social Work*, Routledge: Oxford, pp.155–80.

(1989) 'What does Training have to Offer to Interpersonal Work?', *The Treatment of Child Sexual Abuse*, NSPCC: London.

(1992) 'Social Work Interventions', *Child Abuse Review*, 1 (April) pp.19–32.

(1993) 'Case Management: Does Social Work have a Future?' (paper), Annual Social Services Conference of AMA, ACC & ADSS.

(1993) 'Informal Social Care: Implications for Formal Care',
Hobman D. (ed.), *Uniting Generations*, Age Concern: London,
pp.69–83.

(1994) 'Paid and Unpaid Work: Women who Care for Adult
Dependents', Evetts J., *Women and Career: Themes and Issues in
Advanced Industrial Societies*, Longman: London, pp.87–99.

(1994) 'Social Work in the 1990s: Empowerment, Fact or
Fiction?', Page R. & Baldwin J. (eds), *Social Policy Review* 6,
pp.170–89.

(1994) 'Where now for Interprofessional Work?, Leatheard A.
(ed.), *Going Inter-professional, Working Together for Health and
Welfare*, Routledge: Oxford, pp.123–35.

(1995) 'Case Conferences in Child Protection', James A. &
Wilson K. (eds), *Handbook of Child Protection*, Baillière
Tindall: Oxford, pp.227–41.

(1995) 'The Problems of Vulnerable Children and Adults',
*Proceedings of the International Conference on Family and
Community Care*, Hong Kong Council of Social Services:
Hong Kong, pp.27–30.

(1995) 'What is the Future for Social Work?', *Social Work in
the mid-1990s: Caring with Confidence* (pamphlet), British
Association for Social Work.

(1996) 'Community Care: Concepts and Theories' (in Mandarin),
Theory, Policy and Practice of Community Care, University of
Peking: Beijing, pp.20–28.

(1996) 'Concluding Reflections', Clough R. (ed.), *The Abuse of
Care*, Whiting & Birch: London.

(1996) 'Elder Protection in the Community: What can we Learn
from Child Protection?, HMSO: London.

(1996) 'Emotional Abuse and Neglect: a Time for Reappraisal',
Child and Family Social Work, 1 (1: January) pp.13–18.

(1996) 'Foreword', Waterhouse L. (ed.), *Child Abuse and Child
Abusers*, Jessica Kingsley: London.

(1996) 'Old People's Empowerment', Parsloe P. (ed.), *Pathways to
Empowerment*, Venture Press: New York.

(1998) 'Children in Need and Abused: Interprofessional and Interagency Responses', Stevenson O. (ed.), *Child Welfare in the UK*, Blackwell Science: Oxford, pp.100–20.

(1998) 'Fifty Years of Services to Children in Need of Care: What have We Learnt for Tomorrow?', Lucy Faithfull Memorial Lecture, Barnardo's, Ilford, Essex.

(1998) 'It was More Difficult than We Thought: a Reflection on 50 Years of Child Welfare Practice', *Child and Family Social Work*, 3 (3) pp.153–61.

(1998) 'Neglect: where now? Some reflections', *Child Abuse Review*, 7 pp.111–15.

(1998) 'Social Work with Children and Families', Stevenson O. (ed.), *Child Welfare in the UK*, Blackwell Science: Oxford, pp.79–99.

(1999) 'Elder Protection in Residential Care: What can we Learn from Child Protection?', HMSO: London.

(1999) 'Old People at Risk', Parsloe P. (ed.), *Risk Assessment in Social Care and Social Work*, Jessica Kingsley: London, pp.210–16.

(1999) 'The Protection of Vulnerable People from Abuse: Moral and Professional Dilemmas' (paper), *Transactions of the Leicester Literary and Philosophical Society*, 96 pp.16–17.

(2000) 'The Mandate for Inter-agency and Interprofessional Work & Training', Charles M. & Hendry E. (eds), *Training Together to Safeguard Children*, NSPCC: London, pp.5–13.

(2003) 'The Future of Social Work', Lymbery M. & Butler S. (eds), *Social Work Ideals and Practice Realities*, Palgrave Macmillan: Basingstoke.

(2004) 'Foreword', Taylor J. & Daniel B., *Child Neglect: Practice Issues for Health & Social Care*, Jessica Kingsley: London.

(2004) 'Working Together in Cases of Neglect: Key Issues', Taylor J. & Daniel B., *Child Neglect: Practice Issues for Health & Social Care*, Jessica Kingsley: London, pp.97–112.

(2005) 'Genericism and Specialisation: the Story since 1970', *British Journal of Social Work*, 35 (5) pp.569–86.

(2005) 'Foreword', Bower M. (ed.), *Psychoanalytic Theory for Social Work Practice: Thinking under Fire*, Routledge: Oxford.

(2007) 'Ethnicity and Caregiving: A case study in Great Britain', Paoletti I. (ed.), *Family Care Giving for Older Disabled People: Relational and Institutional Issues*, Nova Science Publications: New York, pp.393–406.

(2007) 'Where are We Now?', James A. & Wilson K. (eds), *Child Protection Handbook*, Baillière Tindall: Edinburgh, pp.532–49.

(2008) 'Neglect as an Aspect of the Mistreatment of Elderly People', *Journal of Adult Protection* 10 (1: February) pp.24–35.

(2012) 'Responses to antisocial youth: Does Donald Winnicott have messages for us today?', Reeves C. (ed.), *Broken Bounds: Contemporary Reflections on the Antisocial Tendency*, Karnac Books: London.